R. Gupta's®

JAMMU AND KASHMIR

UNION TERRITORY

General Knowledge

Including

Ladakh (UT) with Latest Facts & Data

by

**Dr. M.S. Ansari &
RPH Editorial Board**

2021 EDITION

Ramesh Publishing House, New Delhi

Published by
O.P. Gupta *for* Ramesh Publishing House

Admin. Office
12-H, New Daryaganj Road, Opp. Officers' Mess,
New Delhi-110002 ☎ 23261567, 23275224, 23275124

E-mail: info@rameshpublishinghouse.com
Website: www.rameshpublishinghouse.com

Showroom
● Balaji Market, Nai Sarak, Delhi-6 ☎ 23253720, 23282525
● 4457, Nai Sarak, Delhi-6, ☎ 23918938

Book Code: R-1605

ISBN: 978-93-89480-27-6

HSN Code: 49011010

CONTENTS

WHO'S WHO

GIRISH CHANDRA MURMU :
FIRST Lt. GOVERNOR OF JAMMU & KASHMIR (UT)

Girish Chandra Murmu

Girish Chandra Murmu took oath as the first Lieutenant Governor of Jammu and Kashmir on Oct. 31, 2019 following the bifurcation of the state into two union territories.

Murmu is a 1985-batch Gujarat Cadre IAS officer and was appointed as Secretary, Department of Expenditure in March 2019. Born on 21 November 1959, Murmu, a native of Odisha, had worked closely with Prime Minister Narendra Modi in Gujarat as his additional principal secretary during his tenure as chief minister. He served as expenditure secretary at the Centre before getting appointed as Lieutenant Governor of Jammu and Kashmir.

R.K. MATHUR :
FIRST Lt. GOVERNOR OF LADAKH (UT)

Radha Krishna Mathur

Retired IAS officer Radha Krishna Mathur took oath as the first Lt. Governor of union territory of Ladakh on October 31, 2019. He retired as the Chief Information Commissioner of India (CIC) in November 2018. Mathur had retired as the India's Defence Secretary, two years after being appointed to the post on 25 May 2013. He was also the Defence Production Secretary of India, Micro, Small and Medium Enterprises Secretary of India and the Chief Secretary of Tripura.

GITA MITTAL:
CHIEF JUSTICE OF J&K HIGH COURT

Gita Mittal

On 11th August, 2018 Justice Gita Mittal became the first-ever woman Chief Justice of Jammu and Kashmir High Court. She is the first woman for the field of law and justice to be conferred the 'Nari Shakti Puraskar' India's highest civilian honour for women.

JAMMU AND KASHMIR AFTER REORGANISATION ACT, 2019

1. People from other states will now be eligible to serve and purchase land.
2. Legislative Assembly duration in Union Territory of J&K will be 5 years.
3. There will be Common HC for J&K, and Ladakh UTs.
4. There will be Single citizenship only.
5. Tricolour flag will be the only flag to hoisted in Jammu & Kashmir (UT) and Ladakh (UT).
6. Provisions of the Indians Constitution are applicable in the State.
7. UT Administration will have to frame the rules of the services of State cadre and other officers as number of employees from Ladakh are posted in Jammu and Kashmir divisions and vice versa.
8. Jammu and Kashmir Police will come under control of the Union Home Ministry.
9. The process for fresh delimitation will be carried out be setting up a Delimitation Commission.
10. J&K, Reorganization Bill comes into forces and J&K and Ladakh are declared as UTs.
11. No permission will be required to set up industry and non-locals will be eligible to apply for jobs in the UTs unless the administration imposes a cap, with effect from 31st Oct. 2019.
12. There will be no separate Constitution.
13. West Pakistani refugees and Valmikis, who had been denied state subject right even after 72 years of settlement in the State, will be equal stakeholders now.
14. Leh and Kargil districts will have Autonomous Councils, Municipalities and Panchayats. It may be mentioned here that law and order of the UTs is directly controlled by the Central.
15. UT can't make laws pertaining to Law and Orders, Police.
16. UT of Jammu and Kashmir to have only nine Ministers.
17. UT Ladakh to have Advisors.
18. PSC for J&K UT, UPSC for Ladakh.
19. 4 RS members to continue with their term.
20. With abrogation of Article 370, Jammu and Kashmir is as much part of India as all other States.
21. Article 360 (Financial Emergency) will be applicable.
22. Minorities will be eligible for reservation in services.

CURRENT AFFAIRS

J&K and Ladakh are Now Union Territories

Ending Jammu and Kashmir's special status in the Indian Union, the BJP government extended all provisions of the Constitution to the State in one go, downsized the State into two Union Territories and allowed all citizens to vote and buy property in the State. The Union Territory (UT) of Jammu and Kashmir will have a Lieutenant Governor and the maximum strength of its Assembly will be of 107 seats, which will be further enhanced to 114 after a delimitation exercise according to the act passed by Parliament on August 6, 2019. Twenty-four seats of the Assembly

<table>
<tr><td>WHAT IT MEANS</td></tr>
<tr><td>

- J&K will now have no separate flag or Constitution. Tenure of assembly will be for 5 years, not 6; Indian Penal Code will replace Ranbir Penal Code.
- People from other states are now eligible to purchase land and properties. Non-permanent residents can permanently settle in state.
- Outsiders can now be employed in state govt and companies and be eligible for scholarships in state-run educational institutions.
- RTI Act will be applicable in J&K.

</td></tr>
</table>

continue to remain vacant as they fall under Pakistan-occupied Kashmir (PoK).

The UT of Ladakh will have Kargil and Leh districts. There shall be a Council of Ministers in the successor UT of J&K consisting of not more than 10 per cent of the total number of members in the Legislative Assembly, with the Chief Minister as the head to aid and advise the Lieutenant Governor in the exercise of his functions in relation to matters with respect to which the Legislative Assembly has power to make laws. The new UT would have reservation in the Assembly seats.

As per the Act the Lieutenant Governor of the successor UT of J&K may nominate two members to the Legislative Assembly to give representation to women, if in his opinion women are not adequately represented in the Legislative Assembly. The Act said the Lok Sabha would have five seats from the UT of J&K, while Ladakh would have one seat. Jammu and Kashmir will be the largest union territory (UT) in the country in terms of area once it is carved out, following the Centre's move to bifurcate the state. Ladakh will be the second largest UT after it comes into force. With this, the total number of UTs in the country will go up to nine—J&K, Ladakh, Delhi,

<table>
<tr><td>FIRST TIME A STATE HAS BECOME A UT</td></tr>
<tr><td>

There have been earlier instances of a category C state (as former chief commissioners' territories were classified at the time of adoption of the Constitution) becoming a UT. But this is the first time after the 1956 states' reorganisation that a full-fledged state has been relegated to a UT (or two).

</td></tr>
</table>

Puducherry, Diu and Daman, Dadra and Nagar Haveli, Chandigarh, Lakshadweep and Andaman and Nicobar Islands. Currently, only two UTs—Delhi and Puducherry—have Legislative Assemblies. With addition of J&K, the number will go up to three. UTs with Legislative Assemblies have Lt Governors.

Article 370: Article 370 was incorporated in Part XXI (temporary provisions with respect to the State of Jammu and Kashmir) of the Constition. The state's constituent assembly had wanted only those aspects of the Indian Constitution that reflected what Hari Singh had signed away. Besides Article 1, it was the only other article of the Indian Constitution that automatically applied to J&K. The other provisions of the Indian statute could apply to the state only if its constituent assembly concurred. Article 370 provided Jammu & Kashmir with special status, allowing it its own state constitution. The Union of India could legislate/act only in defence, foreign affairs and communications. Since the 1950s, there have been afforts to pull the state into a deeper embrace with the Union, but Art 370 was strengthened when Sheikh Abdullah, who had become the second Prime Minister of J&K in 1948 and was later dismissed, came to an agreement—after spells of detention — with Prime Minister Indira Gandhi in 1975.

35A Defines who is a Permanent Resident: Article 35A was made part of the Indian Constitution in 1954, through a presidential order — through its genesis goes back to early 20th century Dogra apprehensions of an influx from Punjab, which they feared would change the state's demographic and land ownership patterns. The article, which defines who is a permanent resident of J&K and lays down laws restricting property purchase and ownership to such permanent residents, also discriminated against women, depriving them of their state subject rights if they married non-permanent residents.

Administrative Council of J&K UT Constituted

The UT administration on November 19, 2019 constituted an Administrative Council, headed by the Lt-Governor as its chairman and his Advisers as members, to dispose of the cases of various kinds, comprising those involving legislation, including the issue of ordinances. According to a government order, the Chief Secretary would function as Secretary to the Administrative Council. The Administrative Secretaries of the Departments of Finance, Planning, Development & Monitoring, General Administration, Law or of any other department would be invited to the meetings of the council as required by it.

2 Advisers to J&K L-G Appointed

In a bid to expedite restoration of normalcy in the newly-created Union Territory of Jammu and Kashmir, the home ministry on November 14, 2019 appointed two advisors to the Lt Governor Girish Chandra Murmu. The new advisors are former IAS officer KK Sharma and retired IPS officer Farooq Khan. The two were also advisors to former Governor Satya Pal Malik when he was Governor of J&K when it was a full State before October 31, 2019.

J&K Upper House Abolished

The bicameral (two-tier) legislature in Jammu and Kashmir came to an end on October 17, 2019 with the government abolishing 62-year-old Legislative Council, the Upper House of Legislature. The council was abolished under Section 57 of the Jammu and Kashmir Reorganisation Bill, 2019, introduced in the Rajya Sabha on August 5, 2019 and subsequently passed by both Houses of Parliament.

J&K Block Development Council Polls

Over 200 Independents were elected to the post of chairperson in the first-ever Block Development Council (BDC) elections in Jammu and Kashmir, with the BJP winning in 81 of the 310 blocks. The Congress, the National Conference and the PDP stayed away from the elections, the first after abrogation of the state's special status, because of continued detention of their leaders. Elections were held in 283 blocks on October 24, 2019 as twenty-seven candidates were elected unopposed.

Salary Bonanza for J&K and Ladakh

Government employees of the new Union Territories of Jammu and Kashmir and Ladakh will get salaries and other benefits as per the recommendation of the 7th Central Pay Commission from October 31, the Union Home Ministry said on October 22, 2019. The move will benefit 4.5 lakh government employees working in the UTs of J&K and Ladakh.

J&K Panchayat Members to Get Protection, ₹ 2-Lakh Cover

Union Home Minister Amit Shah on September 3, 2019 assured a panchayat delegation from Jammu and Kashmir that those vulnerable to threats from terrorists would get police protection and an insurance cover of ₹ 2 lakh each.

J & K and Ladakh (UTs) : At a Glance

Strategically located Jammu and Kashmir and Ladakh (UTs) constitutes the northern most extremity of India.

Situated between 32.15 degree and 37.05 degree north latitude and 72.35 degree and 83.20 degree east longitude, the total area of the both UTs is 2,22,236 sq. kms including 78114 sq kms under the illegal occupation of Pakistan and 37,555 sq kms under that of China, of which Pakistan illegally handed over 5180 sq kms to China. The J&K and Ladakh are bounded by Pakistan, Afghanistan and China from the West to the East. Length from N—S is 640 kms. and length from E—W is 480 kms.

The countries bordering the both UTs are—Pakistan, Afghanistan and China. The neighbouring states to both UTs are— (a) Punjab; (b) Himachal Pradesh.

The both UTs are well connected with rest of the country by air, rail and road. The Indian Airlines and private airlines operate regular flights to Srinagar, Jammu and Leh.

The National Highway 1-A connects the capital cities of Srinagar and Jammu with rest of the country. There are daily passenger trains connecting Jammu with most of the major cities of the country.

The J&K (UT) consists of 20 districts and Ladakh (UT) consists 2 districts divided in tehsils, blocks, Urban Agglomerations, towns and notified area committee, and villages.

Important Facts

• **Date of Formation:** 31st October, 2019
• **Capital:** **Jammu & Kashmir** : Srinagar (Summer); Jammu (Winter) **Ladakh** : Leh
• **Languages:** Urdu, Kashmiri, Dogri, Pahari, Ladakhi, Balti, Punjabi, Gujri and Dadri
• **Population (Census 2011):** 1,25,41,302, *Males:* 66,40,662, *Females:* 59,00,640.
• **Percentage to total Population of India (2011):** 1.04

- **Decadal Growth of Population (2001-2011):** 23.64%
- **Sex Ratio:** 889 (Females per 1000 males)
- **Area:** 2,22,236 sq. km.
- **Population Density:** 124 (persons per sq. km)
- **Population Below Poverty Line:** 21.63%
- **Total Forest Area:** 22,538 sq. km.
- **Net Area Irrigated:** 325.08 thousand hectares
- **Literacy Rate:** 67.17% (Males – 76.75%, Females – 56.43%)
- **Lok Sabha Constituencies:** 6 (J&K 5, Ladakh 1)
- **Total Road Length:** 27,778 km.
- **Post Offices (2016):** 1701
- **Smallest district of J&K (in area):** Shopian
- **Number of Villages:** 6,551
- **Number of towns:** 86
- **Number of Districts** • **J&K:** 20 • **Ladakh:** 2
- **Muslim Population:** 66.97%
- **Hindu Population:** 29.63%
- **Budhists Population:** 1.36%
- **Sikhs Population:** 2.03%
- **Official Language of the State:** Urdu
- **Biggest Salt Water Lake:** Pangoney (Ladakh)
- **Biggest Fresh Water Lake:** Wular (Bandipora)
- **Biggest Glacier:** Kolahoi (Pahalgam)
- **Biggest Power Project:** Salal Hydel (690 MW)
- **Biggest Cascade:** Aharabal
- **Biggest Golf Course:** Gulmarg
- **Biggest Mosque:** Jamia Masjid (Srinagar)
- **Biggest Temple:** Raghunath Mandir (Jammu)
- **Highest Town:** Leh (11,500 ft above sea level)
- **Highest Pass:** Khardungla between Leh and N Waral (14000 ft above seal level)

- **Highest Airport:** Leh (11,500 ft above sea level)
- **Highest Peak:** Nanga Parbat (26,620 ft above sea level)
- **Highest Lake:** Pangong (Leh, Ladakh)
- **Longest River:** Indus River
- **Longest Road Tunnel:** Chenani-Nashri Tunnel (9.2 km)
- **Longest Highway:** Srinagar—Leh (434 km)
- **Longest River rout:** Khanabal to Khadanyar on Jhelum River
- **Coldest Place:** Dras (Kargil)
- **Deepest Lake:** Manasbal (Ganderbal)
- **Highest Annual Rainlfall:** Ramnagar (Udhampur)
- **Oldest Hydel Power Project:** Mohra
- **Oldest Fort:** Bahu Fort (Jammu)

❏ ❏ ❏

 **Important Dates of J & K**

Dates		Events
BC		
250	:	The great Indian king Ashoka conquered Kashmir.
250	:	Buddhism came to Kashmir.
AD		
95	:	Vikramaditya Harsha occupied the throne of Kashmir.
629-631	:	The Chinese pilgrim Hieun-Tsang visited Kashmir.
712	:	Mohammad-Bin-Qasim invaded Kashmir.
949	:	Gupta dynasty was founded by Parva Gupta in Kashmir.
1149-1150	:	Ancient book on history of Kashmir 'Rajatrangi' completed.
1339	:	Hindu rule was overthrown by Muslim adventurer Shah Mir.
1393	:	Hazrat Mir Mohammad Hamdani (RA) visited Kashmir.
1420	:	Sultan Zain-ul-Aabidin (Badshah) ascended the throne of Kashmir.
1530	:	Kashmir was attacked by Mughals.
1561	:	Chak dynasty was founded by Ghazi Chak.
1578	:	Yousuf Shah-e-Chak ascended the throne of Kashmir.
1588	:	The great Mughal emperor Akbar occupied Kashmir.
1592	:	Yousuf Shah died in Bihar.
1753	:	End of Mughal rule in Kashmir.
1819	:	Kashmir passed into the hands of Sikhs and became a part of Lahore.
1846	:	"Treaty of Amritsar" between British and Gualab Singh was concluded.
1877	:	High Court was established.
1881	:	Modern education started in Kashmir.
1885	:	Partap Singh became the Maharaja of Kashmir.
1920	:	Begar was completely abolished.
1922	:	Banihal Cart road connecting Jammu and Srinagar was thrown open to traffic.
1907	:	Silk factory was established at Srinagar.
1925	:	Maharaja Partap Singh passed away.
1932	:	All J&K Muslim Conference was launched.

Dates		Events
1932	:	Launching of Civil Disobedience Movement by Muslim Conference.
1934	:	Legislative Assembly called Praja Sabha was established.
1938	:	J&K bank was established.
1939	:	Muslim Conference changed into National Conference.
1942	:	Jammu and Kashmir Jamat-I-Islami founded.
1946	:	National Conference launched 'Quit Kashmir Movement'.
15 Oct. 1947	:	Justice Mehar Chand Mahajan sworn-in as the Prime Minister of Jammu and Kashmir.
22 Oct. 1947	:	Armed tribesmen entered in the state with the support of Pakistan troops.
26 Oct. 1947	:	Maharaja Hari Singh signed instrument of accession to India.
30 Oct. 1947	:	Maharaja Hari Singh appointed Sheikh Mohammad Abdullah as the Head of the Emergency Administration.
5 March 1948	:	Maharaja announced Interim Government with Sheikh Mohammad Abdullah as Prime Minister.
1 July 1948	:	Radio Kashmir, Srinagar inaugurated.
2 Nov. 1948	:	Jammu and Kashmir University established.
27 June 1949	:	Indo-Pak cease-fire agreement signed at Karachi.
17 Oct. 1949	:	Article 370 of the Union constitution adopted.
13 July 1950	:	Revolutionary land reforms adopted. Property of land-lords transferred to tillers.
5 May 1952	:	First regular budget presented to constitution-cum-legislative assembly.
24 July 1952	:	PM Nehru announced special position (status) for J&K under Delhi Agreement.
17 Nov. 1952	:	Karan Singh took over as Sadar-i-Riyasat.
14 May 1954	:	Union constitution extended to the state with exceptions and modification.
31 Dec. 1954	:	Public service recruitment board established.
1 April 1956	:	J&K first five year plan of Rs. 1151.71 lakhs launched.
14 July 1956	:	GSI (Geological Survey of India) established office in Srinagar.
22 Dec. 1956	:	Jawahar Tunnel opened.
26 Jan. 1957	:	State constitution came into force.
2 Sept. 1957	:	State PSC set up in place of recruitment board.
24 Oct. 1958	:	J&K Academy of Art, Culture and Languages established.
26 Jan. 1959	:	J&K High Court brought at par with other High Courts in India.
1 Feb. 1960	:	J&K minerals limited established.
26 Apl. 1961	:	Maharaja Hari Singh passed away in Bombay at the age of 64.
20 Oct. 1962	:	China launched attack in Ladakh.
26 Oct. 1962	:	National emergency declared due to China's attack.
23 May 1963	:	Foundation stone of State's first Thermal Project at Kalakate laid.
30 March 1965	:	State constitution amended; Sadar-i-Riyasat and Prime Minister renamed as Governor and Chief Minister, respectively.

Dates		Events
5 August 1965	:	Pakistan pushed armed guirellas into Kashmir.
11 Sept. 1965	:	Cease fire came into force.
9 Aug. 1969	:	Panchayat election held in Kashmir for the first time.
5 Sept. 1969	:	Jammu University created as a separate University.
30 Jan. 1971	:	Indian Airline plane hijacked to Lahore during its flight from Srinagar to Jammu.
3 Dec. 1971	:	Pakistan attacked India; National emergency declared.
11 Dec. 1972	:	India and Pakistan approved line of control in J&K.
14 Aprl. 1983	:	Prime Minister Mrs. Indira Gandhi laid Foundation stone of Jammu-Udhampur Rail link project.
26 Aprl. 1984	:	Jagmohan took over as Governor of J&K.
2 Feb. 1987	:	State was put on ISTD, connected with several countries.
11 May 1987	:	Hangul declared state animal.
4 Feb. 1988	:	Assembly seats increased from 76 to 87.
1 Aug. 1988	:	Initial signs of militancy.
7 Oct. 1989	:	Ladakh granted Scheduled Tribes status.
8 Dec. 1989	:	Rubia Syed abducted.
18 July 1990	:	Kashmir valley declared disturbed area.
1 June 1991	:	Umar Farooq become the new Mir Waiz of Kashmir.
19 Mar. 1994	:	Former Speaker, J&K Legislative Assembly, Wali Mohammad Itoo gunned down by militants in Jammu.
4 July 1994	:	'Harkat-ul-Ansar' (a millitant outfit) banned Amarnath Yatra.
8 Jan. 1995	:	J&K declared backward State under the new industrial policy.
9 May 1995	:	Chrar-i-Sharief town set ablaze by militants.
27 Aug. 1995	:	State Government announced surrender-cum-rehabilitation policy for millitants.
2 Oct. 1995	:	Mid day meal scheme launched.
6 Jan. 1997	:	Govt. announcement setting up of the state Human Rights Commission.
8 Aug. 1998	:	Govt. set up 5-member state Human Rights Commission.
31 Dec. 1999	:	3 dreaded millitants Maulana Masood Azhar, M.A.Zargar and A.Umar released and exchanged with the passengers and crew members of 1C-814, which was hijacked from Kathmandu to Kandhar.
14 May 2002	:	Millitants attacked at Kaluchak killing 30 persons.
9 Oct. 2002	:	Assembly elections result declared; Congress won 20 seats, NC 26, PDP-16, BJP-1, and others 23.
Aug. 2003	:	Mobile service launched in J&K.
17 June 2004	:	Indo European round table conference held in Kashmir.
Aug. 2004	:	Permanent Resident disqualification bill defeated in J&K assembly.
2005	:	Civic election held after 27 years.
7 Aprl. 2005	:	Karvan-E-Aman, A bus service introduced between Srinagar and Muzaffarabad.

Dates		Events
13 Aprl. 2005	:	Prime Minister flagged off Uttar Sampark Kranti, A train between Jammu and Udhampur.
19 June 2005	:	72 crores proposed in annual action plan for Budgam district.
8 Oct. 2005	:	Massive earthquake triggered in Uri and Karnah Tehsil of Kashmir whose epicentre was at Muzaffarabad (POK), killing approximately 800 people and rest rendered homeless. It was 7.6 on Richter scale.
2 Nov. 2005	:	Gulam Nabi Azad sworn in as Chief Minister of the J&K State.
6 Jan. 2006	:	The Union Cabinet approve renaming the civil enclave at Leh as Kushok Bakula Rimpochhe Airport.
31 Jan. 2006	:	J&K cabinet approve ₹ 214 crore Mughal Road contract.
16 Feb. 2006	:	Jammu University host South Asia Youth Festival.
23 Feb. 2006	:	Maharashtra and Jammu and Kashmir entered tourism alliance. State commission for backward classes presented annual plan report.
6 July 2006	:	Eight new districts (Four each in Kashmir and Jammu) were created by the coalition government.
3 Sept. 2006	:	Baig formally resign as Dy. CM.
17 Oct. 2006	:	J&K gets seven FM channels of All India Radio.
June 2007	:	First major International Film festival takes off in Kashmir.
Apr. 2008	:	Army gets First Muslim Major General from Kashmir. Srinagar-Leh Highway opens to traffic.
June 2008	:	The longest 284-metre bridge with 250-metre approach roads at Bemina in Kashmir Valley connecting Srinagar with Budgam district dedicated to the public.
11 Oct. 2008	:	Prime Minister Manmohan Singh flagged off the first ever train service in the Kashmir Valley from the Nowgam railway station.
5 Jan. 2009	:	Omar Abdullah sworn in as the 11th Chief Minister of the J&K State.
17 Aug. 2010	:	Prime Minister Manmohan Singh announced a ₹125 crore relief for the flood-ravaged Leh from the PM Relief Fund.
7 March 2011	:	J&K Finance Minister Abdur Rahim Rather presented a zero deficit budget.
6 March 2012	:	J&K Finance Minister Abdur Rahim Rather presented the annual budget worth ₹33,853 crore for the financial year 2012-13.
22 Feb. 2013	:	The First State Vigilance Commission in Jammu and Kashmir has become functional.
4 March 2014	:	Jammu & Kashmir assembly passed Panchayati Raj Bill.
1 March 2015	:	Mufti Mohammad Sayeed sworn-in as 12th J&K CM; Nirmal Singh Deputy CM.
7 January 2016	:	J&K CM Mufti Mohammad Sayeed died.
4 April 2016	:	Mehbooba Mufti sworn-in as 13th J&K CM; Nirmal Singh Deputy CM.

2 April 2017	:	Prime Minister Narendra Modi inaugurated country's longest Chenani-Nashri road tunnel.
June 2018	:	BJP government pulls out of alliance with PDP.
November 2018:		Governor Satya Pal Malik dissolves legislative assembly.
February 2019	:	A vehicle loaded with explosives crashes into an Indian paramilitary convoy, killing 40 personnel. India carries out retributive strikes on terror camps across the LoC in Pakistan's Balakot region. An Indian Air Force pilot captured by Pakistan and later released.
May 2019	:	The BJP returns to power for a second term in India.
July 2019	:	US president Donald Trump offers to mediate the Kashmir issue between India and Pakistan.
August 4, 2019	:	Prominent Kashmiri leaders, including former chief ministers Omar Abdullah and Mehbooba Mufti, placed under house arrest. Internet and mobile services curtailed, and section 144, which prevents a gathering of more than four people in public spaces, imposed.
August 5, 2019	:	Home minister Amit Shah proposes a presidential order to repeal Article 370 and 35A. J&K to be bifurcated as two union territories of Ladakh (centrally administered) and J&K (with its legislative assembly). Opposition parties protest in parliament; complete shutdown in Kashmir valley.
October 31, 2019:		Jammu and Kashmir, Ladakh became Union Territories. Girish Chander Murmu and R.K. Mathur were sworn in as the first Lt. Governor of Jammu & Kashmir and Ladakh respectively.

❑ ❑ ❑

3 | History

Kashmir is perhaps, to possess an authentic account of its history from the very earliest period. This past account of the valley, its culture and traditions, rise and fall of various Kingdoms, victory and defeats of the people have been noted carefully, yet critically by the sons of its soil. True it is, that the Kashmiriat literature is very rich in information about Kashmir.

The beauty and the salubrious climate of the valley was known even from the ancient times. The mythological traditions supported fully by the research of geologists confirm that the valley originally was a huge lake called "Satisar", (the land of goddess Sati, consort of Lord Shiva) and its waters were blocked near Baramulla (ancient Varahmulla). In the words of Sir Francis Young Husband, "The huge lake must have been twice the length and three times the width of the lake of Geneva, completely encircled by snowy mountains as high, and higher than Mount Blank, while in the immediately following glacial period, mighty glaciers came wending down to the Sindh, Lidder, and other valleys even to the edge of water."

Kashmir's greatest historian Kalhan writes about his native land "It is a country where the sun shines mildly, being the place created by Rishi Kashyap, for his glory - big and lofty houses, learning, Saffron, icy cool water and grapes rare in Heaven are plentiful here - Kailash is the best place in the three worlds (Tn-bk), Himalayas the best place in Kailash, and Kashmir the best place in Himalayas". Our immortal Sanskrit poet Kalidas writes about the valley;

"The place is more beautiful than the heaven and is the benefactor of supreme bliss and happiness. It seems to me that I am taking a bath in the lake of nectar here."

Sir Walter Lawrence writes "The valley is an emerald set in pearls; a land of lakes, clear streams, green turf, magnificent trees and mighty mountains where the air is cool, and the water sweet, where men are strong, and women vie with the soil in fruitfulness. "He further writes that the valley contains everything which should make life enjoyable. There is sport varied and excellent; there is scenery for the artist and the layman, mountain for the mountaineer, flower for the Botanist, a vast field for the Geologist and magnificent ruins for the archaeologist.

PRE-HISTORIC TIMES

According to the oldest extant book on Kashmir, "Nilmat Puran", in the Satisar lived a demon called Jalod Bowa, who tortured and devoured the people, who lived near mountain slopes. Hearing the suffering of the people, a great saint of our country, Kashyap by name, came to the rescue of the people here. After performing penance for a long time, the saint was blessed, and he was able to cut the mountain near Barahmulla, which had blocked the water of the lake from flowing into the plains below. The lake was drained, the land appeared, and the demon was killed. The saint encouraged people from India to settle in the valley. The people named the valley as Kashyap-Mar and Kashyap-Pura. The name Kashmir also implies land desicated from water: "ka" (the water) and shimeera (to desicate). The ancient Greeks called it "Kasperia" and the Chinese pilgrim Hien-Tsang who visited the valley around 631 A.D. called it KaShi-Mi-Lo". In modern times the people of Kashmir have shortened it into "Kasheer" in their tongue.

Regarding pre historic times Dr Sunil Chandra Ray writes Pre-historic explorations have discovered the occurence of quatemary Glacial cycles in the valley. The chief Geological formation of the ice-age here are the lacustrine deposits called the "Karewas", which overlay the terminal moraines of the first Glaciation and are comprised of two groups, Lower and Upper, differentiated by the moraines of the second Glaciation. The fossil remains of Elphas-hysudrious obtained in the lower 'Karewas' point to lower "Pleistocene age", writes De Teera. The neolithic culture is indicated by the discovery of ground and polished stone axes, hoes, pestle, and bone implements at the well-known megalithic site of Burazahoma, ten miles east of, Srinagar. Burazahoma is famous as one of the only two megalithic sites in the extreme north-west of Indian sub-continent. We do not exactly know the Cultural horizon of the Burazahoma megalithic, nor the Purpose for which they were erected, but the indications are, they were put in places towards the end of the neolithic period at that site, between 400 to 300 B. C."

In 1960, Archaeological Department of the Govt. of India began systematic excavation at this site. Near about the siltbed, pits have been discovered in sections, indicating a settlement of early Pit dwellers whose date has tentatively been fixed at 3000 BC .This is perhaps the only known find of such a settlement in India. It is possible that more valuable data would be found, when extensive surface diggings are completed.

HINDU PERIOD

Kalhana in his book Rajatarangini stated that the history of Kashmir started just before the great Mahabharat war. According to him the first king who ruled over Kashmir is Gonanda, his reign is placed as 653 Kaliera, the traditional date of coronation of King Yudhistira, the eldest brother of the Pandvas, Gonanda was killed in a battle along with his son and at the time of the commencement of the Mahabharat war, Gonanda II was ruling over Kashmir.

Ashoka founded the old city of Srinagar known now as "Pandrethan". At Vijeshwari (modern Bijbehra), he built a Shiva Temple, thus winning the heart of the local population, who were mostly worshippers of Lord Shiva making a gift of the valley to Sangha.

According to local tradition, like Lord Shri Krishna, Lord Buddha is also supposed to have visited Kashmir. After the death of Ashoka, his son Jaluka ascended the throne of Kashmir, and the latter was succeeded by his son King Damodar II, Jaluka was a great king who cleared the valley of oppressing 'Malechas'.

The scholars also, accept the theory that the valley for over two hundred years was ruled by Indo-Greek Kings before the start of "Turushka" (Kushan) rule in the state. Cunningham records a large fund of silver coins of Azes (and Azilies) (coins of Indo-Scythians) on the banks of Vitasta (river Jhelum) in the hills between Varahmulla and Jhelum.

The contact with the Greeks is responsible for the beautiful architectural and sculptural style of old Kashmir temples, and the coinage of later Kashmir Kings has also been influenced by this contact. The three kings mentioned by Kalhan are Huska, Juska, and Kanishka, each of them is credited with the foundation of a town, christened after their respective names: Hushkapura, Jushkapura and Kanishkapura. The Kushan Kings also built many temples and Vihars. Kanishka held the third great council of the Buddhist church at "Kundalvan".

Hien Tsang has given the proceedings of this Council. Nearly 500 Buddhist and Hindu scholars attended this conference, and a learned Kashmir Brahmin Vasumitra presided over its session. Some of the great Buddhist Scholars, who took active part in this council, were Ashvagosha, Nagarjuna, Vasubandu Sangamitra and Jinamitra.

Hiuen-Tsang praises the intellectual caliber of the Kashmir scholars, and considered them as incomparable. The entire proceedings of the conference were inscribed on copper plates in Sanskrit, enclosed in stone boxes, deposited in a Vihar. Like famous Gilgit manuscripts, it is possible that these copper plates may be unearthed in near future, and we would learn much about the rich cultural history of the valley.

In 950, Khemgupta ascended the throne of Kashmir, a man of mediocre ability who married princess Didda, daughter of the ruler of Lohara (Poonch) and granddaughter of the Sahi King of Kabul. In 980 A.D. Didda ascended the throne after the death of her husband. Before her, two other queens had ruled Kashmir namely Yashovati and Sugandha. Didda was a very unscrupulous and willful lady and led a very immoral life. But inspite of these drawbacks, she was an able ruler, who firmly ruled the valley. She died in 1003 A.D. and left the throne of Kashmir to her family in undisputed succession, as her children had died young, she transmitted the crown to Sangramraj, son of her brother Udairaj, the ruler of Lohara (Poonch). It was during her time that Mahmud Gaznavi twice tried to capture the valley but the fort at Lohara, remarkable for its height and strength proved impregnable. The Sultan was obliged to abandon the conquest.

From 1089 - 1101 AD, King Harsha and from 1155-1339, the Kashmir rulers remained busy with intrigues, debauchery, and mutual quarrels. The last Hindu ruler of Kashmir was Udayan Dev. Before his death, he embraced Islam. His death in 1339 paved the way for the establishment of Muslim rule in Kashmir.

MUSLIM PERIOD

After the death of Queen Kota, Shah Mir ascended the throne under the name of Sultan Shamas-ud-din, and his dynasty ruled the state for 222 years. This period is one of the most important in the annals of Kashmir, in as much as Islam was firmly established here. The Shah-Miri dynasty has given us only two rulers, who are worthy of mention. One is Sultan Shihab-ud-din, and the second is the great Sultan Zain-ul-Abidin. The former ascended the throne in 1354, and continued to rule till 1371. He was full of energy, and vigour and he was able to establish his sway over the neighboring countries. His army mainly consisted of Damras, Lavans and the hill tribes of Poonch, Rajapuri and Kishtwar. The important commanders who served under him were both Hindus and Muslims, such as Chandra-Damra, Laula Daniara, Shura, Syed Hassan and Abdul Raina. His two important Hindu ministers were Kota Bhat and Udyashri. At the begining of his reign, he led an army to Sindh and defeated its ruler. While returning he defeated Afgans near Peshawar and then he conquered Kabul, Gazni, Qandhar, Pakhali, Swat and Multan. He invaded Badakshan, and then marched towards Dardistan and Gilgit, which he easily conquered. Then he marched towards Bulochistan and Ladhak. The ruler of Kashgar (central Asia) came with a huge army and Shihab-ud-din whose army was numerically inferior, inflicted a crushing defeat and the Kashgar army was almost wiped out. This led to the annexation of Laddhak and Bultistan, which were claimed by the Kashgar ruler. It is also said that the ruler of Kashmir marched towards Delhi, and on the way conquered Kangra, and then the army of Ferozashah Tughlaq opposed him on the banks of Sutluj. Since the battle between the rulers of the Delhi and Kashmir was indecisive, peace was concluded, and it was agreed that all the territory from Sirhind to Kashmir belonged to the Kashmir ruler. Shihab-ud-din was not only a great conqueror but also an able administrator, and he governed his kingdom with firmness and justice. He was tolerant ruler and treated his Hindu subjects generously.

It is reported that owing to prolonged campaigns he needed money, and his ministers asked him to loot the temples, but he stoutly opposed the proposal, and to quote Jonaraj, he is reported to have said in anger: "Past generation have set-up images to obtain fame, and earn merit, and you propose to demolish them. Some have obtained renown by setting up images of gods, others by worshipping them, some by maintaining them, and you propose demolishing them How great is the enormity of such a deed". The king founded a new town which he called Shihab-ud-din pora, known now as Shadipur(now near sumbal in District Bandipora). He is also said to have erected many mosques and monasteries. Shihab-ud-din can rightly be called the Lalitaditya of medieval Kashmir. During his time Kashmir armies marched to distant lands, and our victorious banners were unfurled on many forts of foreign countries. Thus this great ruler raised Kashmir to great eminence, and power.

The next ruler was Sultan Qutab-ud-din, and in whose time the important event and worth mentioning revolution is the arrival of Iranian sufi saint Mir Sayyed Ali Hamdani, who was the most remarkable personality of the then muslim world. At the time of his third visit he got with himself 700 Syyeds from Hamdan, who were being out to torture by Timur, ruler of Persia. Iranian saint, Mir Syyed Ali Hamadani is known as the founder of Islam in Kashmir. These syyeds established their centres of missonery activities in different parts of the valley. In 1389, Qutab-ud-din died, and he was succeeded by his eldest son Sultan-Sikandar. Shahi-Khan or Sultan Zain-ul-Abidin ascended the throne in 1420 A. D. and ruled upto 1470 A. D. nearly for half a century. His accession to the throne, proved to be the return of a bright and warm day after a cold and a chilly night.

Zain-ul Abidin organized a huge army, and with its help he reconquered the Punjab, Western Tibet, Ladhak and Balti region, Kulu and Ohind (Hazara). The Sultan also maintained cordial and friendly relations with rulers of other countries. The Sheriff of Macca and the Kings of Juan and Egypt sent him presents. The Maharaja of Gwalior, hearing that the Sultan was interested in Music, sent him valuable works on Indian music. There was also an exchange of embassies and gifts between the great Sultan and the rulers of Sindh, Bengal, Tibet, Gujarat, Malwa and Delhi. The Sultan improved the tone of administration which had rudely been shaken. He appointed talented persons in high administrative posts, irrespective of caste or creed. The Sultan had a high sense of justice and no one who committed a crime was spared, however close he was to throne. Many grandees who were favourites of the king, were severly punished when found guilty. The king took keen interest in agriculture and like Lalitaditya and Avantivarman, many canals were dug out in all parts of the Kingdom. Jonraj and Shriva have given details of these canals in their valuable books. Owing to these irrigation works, the draining of marshes and reclamation of large areas for cultivation, Kashmir became self-sufficient in food, and rice was cheap.

In 1470 A. D. the Sultan died and for a long time his death was mourned by the people. Sultan Zain-ul-Abidin's death sounded the death knell of Shah-Miri dynasty. It met the same fate that the Lohara dynasty had met after the death of Jaisimha in 1156. The only important event that took place before the establishment of Chak dynasty was the invasion of Mirza Haider Dughlat who attacked Kashmir from Zogila pass in 1533. Soon he was able to establish his ascendancy in the valley. The Moghul, like Dulchu earlier, killed, looted and plundered the people, and made women and children their slaves. The Sultan of Kashmir, Nazuk Shah, became almost a puppet in his hands. Moghuls were appointed on high posts everywhere, and the Jagirs of Kashmir Noblemen were confiscated. For more than a decade Mirza was the virtual ruler of the valley and he gave peace and orderly Government to the country. He encouraged Kashmir Art and Crafts, and trade and commerce once again thrived in the valley. The last Kashmiri ruler, Sultan Habib Shah, a weakling was deposed by his commander, and nobles raised on throne Gazi Chak, a prominent military General of the time. He was the direct descendant of Lankar Chak who had come to Kashmir towards the close of Hindu rule. The Chak rule began in Kashmir in 1561 and lasted till 1587, when Akbar, the great Moghul Emperor conquered Kashmir.

MUGHAL PERIOD

During the period of Mughal rule from 1587 to 1752, the people enjoyed peace and order. Akbar built a new town near Hariparbat and called it Nagar-Magar and built the massive wall around the hill. The Mughal rulers never came alone, but were always accompanied by hundreds of Nobles, Amirs and Umras, Princes and Army Generals. Jahangir came virtually, under the spell of the scenic beauty of the place, and wherever he found a hill coming down gently to a spring or a grove of majestic Chinar trees or a beautiful lake, he utilized the place for planting a pleasure garden.

Shalimar and Nishat gardens on the banks of Dal Lake, would keep Jahangir's love for natural beauty ever fresh in our memory. Table shows important Mughal gardens from J&K.

Mughal Gardens in J&K

Name of Gardens	Name of the ruler who built it
Shalimar	Jehangir for his beloved wife Noorjahan
Chashmashahi	Shahjahan
Nishat	Jehangir
Harwan	Asif Khan
Pari Mahar	Shahjehan

Important gardens are Shalimar, Harwan and Nishat. All gardens are facing Dal Lake. Aurangazeb visited Kashmir only once in 1665. Because of instability, lack of unity and discriminations of Mughul kings lead to Afghan invasion in 1752. In Kashmir most of the gardens are built by Mughal rulers.

AFGHAN RULE

The rulers of Kabul were great despots, and they ruled all the parts of their kingdom ruthlessly with an iron hand. The cornerstone of their policy was terror. As many as twenty eight Durrani Subedars governed Kashmir during these sixty seven years. Most of the well to do people of the valley were summoned by the Abid Ali Governor Abdullah Khan to his palace, and ordered to surrender all their wealth on pain of death. Their houses were completely sacked, and many people were put to sword. There was complete gloom and despair on every side.

All the prosperity of the valley was gone, and the people could not even move on the streets, for fear of being robbed of even their scanty clothing. Each and everyday for a Kashmiri was a day of struggle and uncertainty. In 1819 the State was added to the Sikh Kingdom of Punjab. The Sikh rule over Kashmir lasted only for a brief span of time, during which the rulers at Lahore were far too pre-occupied at home to pay any attention to the affairs of this outlying province of theirs.

The misery of the people increased due to natural calamities as well, such as premature snow falls, which would destroy a ripe rice crop leading to famines. These famines were followed by diseases like cholera and plague resulting in a heavy loss of life. Thousands of people migrated to India during these hard days, and no wonder the population of the valley came down to two lakhs from nine lakhs.

SIKH RULE

At last the reign of terror broke the patience of the peace loving people, and a deputation of Kashmiris led by Pandit Birbal Dhar, and his son Pandit Rajakak Dhar, left for Lahore and fervently requested Maharaja Ranjit Singh to conquer Kashmir. Three prominent Muslims helped Pandit Birbal Dhar in his escape from the valley. They were Abdul Qadoos Gojwari, Mallick Zulfiqar and Malik Kamgar. In 1819, 30,000 soliders of Maharaja Ranjit Singh attacked Kashmir, defeated the Pathans, and the state became a part of Ranjit Singh's empire. On receipt of the news, Maharaja Ranjit Singh bestowed honours in Dhar family and Lahore was illuminated for three days, Sikh rule lasted for only 27 years and during this period 10 Governors administersd the country one after another, out of whom the last two were Muslims. In the beginning Sikh rule also proved to be oppressive. "It must have been an intense relief", writes Lawrence, "to all classes in Kashmir to see the downfall of the evil rule of Pathan, and to none was the relief greater than to the peasants who had been cruely fleeced by the rapacious sardars of Kabul. I do not mean to suggest that the Sikh rule was benign or good, but it was at any rate better than that of the Pathans". The Sikh rule over Kashmir lasted only for a brief span of time, during which the rulers at Lahore were far too pre-occupied at home to pay any attention to the affairs of this outlying province of theirs. The misery of the people increased due to natural calamities as well, such as premature snow falls, which would destroy a ripe rice crop leading to famines. These famines were followed by diseases like cholera and plague, resulting in a heavy loss of life. Thousands of people migrated to India during these hard days, and no wonder the population of the valley came down to two lakhs from 8 lakhs.

Mr. Ranel Tayler who visited Kashmir in 1846 writes about Kashmir, "The town presents a very miserable apperance. The houses made of wood are tumbling in every direction. The streets are filthy for want of drainage, none of the bazars looked wellfilled and prospseous and altogether my ride made me very unhappy". Moorcraft who visited the valley in 1835 writes, "Everywhere the people were in most abject condition, not one sixteenth of the cultivable land is under cultivation, and the inhabitants are starving. They were in a condition of extreme weakness Villages were half deserted and those who lived there were the semblance of extreme sickness. Villages were filthy and swarming with beggars. The rural folk on the whole were half naked and miserably emaciated and presented a ghostly picture of poverty and starvation". Such was the general condition of the state when Maharaja Ranjit Singh died in 1830. His death was a signal for the mutiny of Sikh Army which become uncontrollable, and plunge entire Punjab into confusion and chaos.

DOGRA PERIOD

Dogras are from Indo-Aryan ethnic group in south Asia. Dogras believed to be suryavanshi Rajputs of chattri origin. They are migrated from Rajputana many centuries ago. They live predominantly in the J&K, Punjab, Himachal Pradesh and North East Pakistan. They speak their own language called Dogri. Most of the Dogras are Hindus, some are Muslims and some are Sikhs. From 1846 to 1949, four Dogra kingdoms are ruled in J&K. The Kashmir accession was started at the time of Maharaja Harising. Table gives names of Dogra rulers of J&K.

List of Dogra Rulers

Gulab Singh	1846 - 1857
Ranbir Singh	1857 - 1885
Partab Singh	1885 - 1925
Hari Singh	1925 - 1949

The two Anglo-Sikh Wars led to the final extinction of Sikh sovereignty in the Punjab and by virtue of the treaties of Lahore and Amritsar the British who had by now become undisputed master of India. The greatest service of the first Dogra ruler is the foundation that he laid for the modern Jammu and Kashmir State. The Maharaja died in 1857 after a rule of 11 years, during which period he laid the foundation of a sound system of administration. He was succeeded by Maharaja Ranbir Singh who ruled from 1857 to 1885.

In 1885 Maharaja Sir Pratap Singh ascended the throne and he ruled for a period of 40 years. The real modernization of the state and several progressive reforms were carried out by him. Sir Walter Lawrence brought the first assessment of land revenue system in the state on scientific lines. The two mountain roads, Jhelum valley road and Banihal Cart were built by linking the state with the rest of India.

A scheme for drainage of the valley reclaiming waste-land and preventing floods by digging flood channels was put into operation. Construction of water reservoir at Harwan and establishment of electric generating plant at Mohra was also undertaken during this period. Two colleges in the state besides large number of education institutions were also established by the order of the Maharaja.

The administrative machinery was completely overhauled. There was development in the means of communication and telegraphs. Telephones and post offices were opened in many places. After the death of Maharaja Pratap Singh his nephew Maharaja Sir Hari Singh ascended the throne in 1925. He continued to govern the state till 1949. Hari Singh was the last ruler of Kashmir. When India got freedom in 1947 the land was divided into two parts- India and Pakistan.

By this time most of the princely states of India were united to form the Indian Union. Kashmir, an independent state under Raja Hari Singh, decided to join India due to great similarity in culture and social aspects. The instrument of accession was signed between Lord Mountbatten and Raja Harisingh in terms of defense, external affairs and rehabilitation of refugees.

The most important thing that had far reaching consequences in the future of the state was the birth of political parties and the growth of political consciousness in the state during this period. But more important was the liberation of the country from the British Yoke in 1947 that ended all the traces of foreign domination, absolutism and autocracy in our country.

❏ ❏ ❏

4 ▶ Geography

LOCATION

Strategically located Jammu & Kashmir and Ladakh UTs constitutes the northern most extremity of India.

Situated between 32.15 degree and 37.05 degree north latitude and 72.35 degree and 83.20 degree east longitude, the total area of the both UTs is 2,22,236 sq. kms including 78114 sq kms under the illegal occupation of Pakistan and 37,555 sq kms under that of China, of which Pakistan illegally handed over 5180 sq kms to China. The both UTs are bounded by Pakistan, Afghanistan and China from the West to the East.

The both UTs are well connected with rest of the country by air, rail and road. The Indian Airlines and private airlines operate regular flights to Srinagar, Jammu and Leh.

The National Highway 1-A connects the capital cities of Srinagar and Jammu with rest of the country. There are daily passenger trains connecting Jammu with most of the major cities of the country.

The Jammu & Kashmir (UT) consists of 20 districts and Ladakh (UT) consists of 2 districts divided in tehsils, blocks, municipalities, towns and notified area committee, and villages.

It has four geographical zones of (1) Sub-mountain and semi-mountain plain known as kandi or dry belt, (2) The Shivalik ranges, (3) The high mountain zone constituting the Kashmir Valley, Pir Panjal range and its off-shoots including Doda, Poonch and Rajouri districts and part of Kathua and Udhampur districts, (4) The middle run of the Indus river comprising Leh and Kargil.

The Jammu & Kashmir and Ladakh comprising three distinct Climatic regions viz. Arctic cold desert areas of Ladakh, temperate Kashmir valley and sub-tropical region of Jammu.

There is a sharp rise of altitude from 1000 feet to 28250 feet above the sea level within State's four degree of latitude.

The climate varies from tropical in Jammu plains to semi-arctic cold in Ladakh with Kashmir and Jammu mountainous tracts having temperate climatic conditions. The annual rainfall also varies from region to region with 92.6 mm in

17

Leh, 650.5 mm in Srinagar and 1115.9 mm in Jammu. A large part of the both UTs forms part of the Himalayan mountains. Both UTs are geologically constituted of rocks varying from the oldest period of the earth's history to the youngest present day river and lake deposits.

PHYSIOGRAPHY

The territory of the both UTs is divided into seven physiographic zones closely associated with the structural components of the western Himalayas. These include:

Plains: The plains of the Jammu region are characterized by interlocking sandy alluvial fans that have been deposited during the Pleistocene age by the streams flowing from the foothills and by a much dissected pediment (eroded bedrock surface) covered by loams and loess (fine deposits of silt).

Foothills: Rising from 2,002 to 7,002 ft, the foothills form the outer and inner zones.

Lesser Himalayas: Composed of Permo-Carboniferous volcanic rocks of granite, gneisses, quartz and states, the Pir Panjal constitutes the first mountain rampart comprising the westermost part of the Lesser Himalayas.

Greater Himalayas: This contains ranges reaching more than 20,013 ft (6,100 m) in altitude. These ranges act as a climatic divide and stop the cold wind coming from Central Asia.

Valley of Kashmir: Between the Pir Panjal and the western end of the Great Himalayan ranges lies a deep asymmetrical basin called the Valley of Kashmir.

Upper Indus Valley: The Valley of the Upper Indus river follows the geological strike (structural trned) westwards from the Tibetan border to the point in the Pakistani sector where, it rounds the great mountainous mass of Nanga Parbat to run southwards in deep gorges cut across the strike. In its upper reaches, gravel terraces flank the river, each tributary builds an alluvial fan in the main valley. The town of Leh stands on such a fan, 11,483 ft (3,500 m) above the sea level.

Karakoam: The Karakoram region contains some of the world's highest peaks. As the altitude rises very much and majestic peaks appear; K_2 (Godwin Austin) the second highest peak in the world (28,264 ft or 8,611 m) occupies the most important position.

KINDS OF SOIL IN JAMMU & KASHMIR

The main three types of soils in our state are:

1. Alluvial Soil: In our state these are very productive and found in Southern plains of Jammu along with valley bottom of Kashmir and along the branches of the Jhelum and Chenab. Rice and wheat are cultivated in these soil. These are formed by sand, silt and mud brought by rivers during floods.

2. Karewa Soil: It is found in form of flat and low mounds. These soils exit in Kashmir and Kishtwar. These soils also exist in Pampore, Mattan, Tral, Kulgam, Qazigund etc. Kerewas are suitable for growing saffron and fruits. These soils are suitable also for almonds, apples, walnuts and pears. These are permeable soils.

3. Hill Soil: These are acidic in nature and don't have much Potash, Phosphorous and lime. These are found above 700 m from sea level. Maize, Pulses, oil seeds etc are cultivated. Orchards of apples, walnut and pear thrive on these soils.

MOUNTAINS AND THEIR PASSES

Kashmir valley is enclosed by high mountain-chains on all sides, except for certain passes and a narrow gorge at Baramulla. There are Shivalik hills towards the south and very lofty mountains in the north, the peaks of which always remain covered with snow. There are volcanic mountain too in the state. Some of the famous mountains and their passes are:

Karakoram and Kyunlum: Both these mountain ranges lie to the north and north-east of the state and spearate it from Russian, Turkistan and Tibet. In the north-west, Hindukush range continues towards Karakoram ranges, where K2 peak, the second highest peak of the world, is situated. Two lofty peaks of Gasherbrum (8,570 m) and Masherbrum (7,827 m) also lie there. People of Ladakh pass through Karakoram pass (5,352 m) and Nubra pass (5,800 m) while going to Chinese Turkistan and Khattan. One can reach Tibet from Ladakh via Kharudangala pass (5,557 m) and Changla pass (5,609 m).

Zaskar: It is about 600 metres above sea level and separates Indus valley from the Valley of Kashmir. It prevents south-west, coastal winds from reaching Kashmir. Ladakh region terminates at Zojila pass (3,529 m), from where begins the Valley of Kahsmir. Poet pass (5,716 m) is also a famous pass in this range.

Nanga Parbat: This range spreads in Gilgit. Its height is 8,107.68 m above sea level and is utterly devoid of vegetation. It was conquered by the Italian mountaineers in 1954. This is now under the unlawful possession of Pakistan.

Amarnath: Amarnath mountain is famous for its holy Amarnath cave, at a height of 5,372 m above sea level. They have to pass Mahagunas pass (1,475 m) on their way to Shri Amarnathji. Gwasharan (5,450 m) is situated in the Lidar valley towards Pahalgam; on it lies the famous glacier Kolahi. Sheshnag mountain also spreads in this valley. It is called Sheshnag as its peaks resemble the heads of seven big snakes.

Toshmaidan: Toshmaidan (4,270 m) and Kajinag (3,700 m) mountains lie in the inner Himalayas. They ramain clad with snow throughout the year, but during summer when the snow melts, the water flows down into the Jhelum river.

Afarwat: This mountain spreads through the Gulmarg valley. The famous spring Alpathar lies on its peak, from which, Nullah Nagal comes out and flows down into the Wular lake.

Pir Panjal: This range separates Kashmir valley from the outer Himalayas and it is about 2,621 km in length and 50 km in breadth. Famous Banihal pass

(2,832 m) lies in the shape of a tunnel on its peak, it remains covered with snow during winter making it impassable. Now at a height of 2,200 m above sea level a new tunnel, namely 'Jawahar Tunnel' has been constructed. The tunnel is 2,825 m long and it was opened for traffic on 22nd Dec, 1956. On the other end of this range lie Baramulla pass (1,582 m) and Hajipir pass (2,750 m). Hajipir joins Punch and Uri. During 1965 Indo-Pak War, the Indian Army had occupied this pass. Later on, it was handed over to Pakistan.

Shivalk: These hills extend from the north of the outer plains to middle mountains of the state reaching heights varying from 600 m to 1,500 m above sea level.

Volcanic Peak: One Volcanic Peak 'Soyamji' (1,860 m) is situated in North Machhipura (Handwara) and the other 'Kharewa peak' lies in Tehsil Pahalgam, which is now dead or extinct; the former, however, continued eruption of Lava for about thirteen months during 1934, is now in dormant state. There is a temple on this peak and many sulphur springs are found at the foot of the hill. These volcanic mountains are the cause of earthquakes in Kashmir. So far, twelve devastating earthquakes have occurred in Kashmir. Of these, the earthquake of 1885 was the most devastating. Hundreds of houses collapsed, thousands of people died and there were cracks in the earth as a result of this earthquake.

5 Climate

Climate exerts a profound influences on the inhabitants of any region. Their social, cultural, economic and other aspects of life are directly or indirectly governed by climate. The climate of the state ragnes from the burning and the scorching heat of the plains of (Jammu Division) to the snow-capped heights of Gulmarg (Kashmir) and the mud peak of Mount Godwin Austin (Ladakh) 28,264 ft above sea level, the second highest in the world. All these represent the three different climatic zones.

CLIMATE OF JAMMU DIVISION

The climatic conditions of Jammu region depends on the division such as (I) Plain region lying to the South of Shivaliks and (II) the mountainous region stretching in the district of Ramban, Udhampur, Kishtwar, Doda, Reasi, Poonch and Rajouri. Broadly speaking the Jammu division is the humid subtropical region and variable seasons are seen due to seasonal winds, monsoons and temperature. The seasons are:

(a) Cold weather or Winter Season (November – February)

(b) Hot weather or Summer Season (March – June)

(c) Rainy Season (June – October)

(i) **Winter Season (November to February):** In this season the coldest month is January. From February the temperature begins to rise and the atmosphere becomes pleasant giving start to spring season.

(ii) **Summer Season (March to June):** From March onwards there is a abrupt rise in the temperature of Jammu which reaches upto its maximum in the month of May and June and Jammu becomes hottest ranging temperature from 38 degree Celsius to 44 degree Celsius. During this period hot dry winds called 'loo' blow which add to the miseries of the people.

(iii) **Rainy Season (June end to 15th September):** From the middle of June monsoons begin to arrive in Jammu. Monsoon rains bring down the temperature but humidity remains quite high which makes the weather quite oppressive. Average rainfall during this season is 65 cm.

CLIMATE OF KASHMIR DIVISION

The climate of the Kashmir division has its own peculiarities linked with the weather mechanism in the subcontinent in general. The seasons/climate of Kashmir are:

(a) Mild summers

(b) Severe winters with snowfall

(c) A mugy weather in July and August

(d) Pleasant spring

(i) **Winter Season (November to February):** Winter season is the coldest season in Kashmir. It begins from November to February. The temperature substantially declines in December. January is the coldest month known as period of kalan chilla for 40 days. Snowfall is maximum in (Doru) South Kashmir and North Kashmir. In winter the sunshine is low and relative humidity remains about 90%.

(ii) **Spring Season (March to Mid May):** It is locally known as Sonth. The day temperature fluctuates between 10 degree Celsius to 20 degree Celsius. The minimum temperature remains around 3 degree Celsius. In the spring season there is steady increase in temperature from April to May.

(iii) **Summer Season (May to September):** During summer season the valley of Kashmir experiences mean maximum and minimum temperatures which fluctuate between 30 degree Celsius and 18 degree Celsius respectively. The neighbouring hill resorts such as Gulmarg and Pahalgam being at higher altitudes records low temperature.

(iv) **Autumn Season (Mid September to October):** This season is a mark of transition from the warm summer to temperate winters. In this season, there is a clear sky with very little rainfall. This season attracts largest number of tourists in the valley from various parts of the country. The people remained busy in collecting the firewood for ensuing winters. After harvesting crop rice, saffron, apple and almonds the Kashmiri arrange the wedding of their sons and daughters.

CLIMATE OF LADAKH

The aforementioned climatic divide does not apply only to Kashmir valley but also to the parts of Jammu which, like Kashmir valley, are subjected to snowfall and a severe winter. Many parts of the Ladakh region are also subjected to heavy snowfall and others to severe dry cold. There is such heavey snowfall on the way to Ladakh from the valley that it remains cut off by road for about 5-6 months every year.

Rivers and Lakes

The main rivers that flow through the Jammu & Kashmir and Ladakh (UTs) are Jhelum, Chenab and Indus. These rivers are of Himalayan origin. The river Indus originates at the Mansarovar lake in Tibet. Some of the lakes in the Jammu & Kashmir region are Manasbal lake, Dal lake and the Wular lake. Rising from a deep spring at Verinag, the Jhelum meanders north-west from the northern slope of the Pir Panjal range through the Valley of Kashmir to the Wular lake.

IMPORTANT RIVERS

The main rivers that flow through the Jammu & Kashmir and Ladakh region are:

Jhelum: The Jhelum is the main waterway of the Valley of Kashmir. It rises from a spring called Verinag from where a number of tributaries join the Jhelum and make it navigable from Khannabal to Wular lake. Its total length in the valley is 177 km.

Ravi: The Ravi river leaves the Himalayas at Basoli and passes close to Kathua near Madhopur where it enters the plain of the Punjab.

Tawi: The Tawi river, draining the outer hill region, flows around the city of Jammu after collecting drainage to the northeast of Jammu in the interior mountains.

Chenab: The Chenab river rises in the Himalayan contour of Lahul and Spiti. Two streams, more or less parallel, the Chandra and the Bhaga form the Chandrabhaga, or the Chenab. It drains the eastern section of the southern slope of Pir Panjal.

Indus: The Indus is another important river, which originates in Tibet near Kashmir border. A considerable portion of this river flows through our neighbouring nations.

Zanskar: The Zanskar river, a north flowing tributary of the Indus river, has two main branches in its upper reaches. First of these, the Doda originates near Pensi-La (4,400 m) mountain pass and flows through the main Zanskar valley. The second branch is formed by two main tributaries, the Kargyag river with its source near the Shingo La (5,091 m) and Tsarap river with its source near the Baralacha-La.

Kishanganga: The Kishanganga or the Neelum river flows through the Kashmir region and enters Pakistan in the Gurais sector of the Line of Control. It meets the Jhelum river north of Muzzafarabad. The controversial Kishanganga Power Project is being constructed on it.

Doda: The Doda river originates from the Drang Drung glacier of the Pensi-La and flows through the state of Ladakh. The river flows into the Padum valley, and joins with the Tsarap river to form the larger river Zanskar.

Dras: The Dras river, a tributary of the Suru river, originates in the Machoi Glacier near the Zozi-La pass.

Shyok: The Shyok river, a tributary of the Indus river, traverses through the Ladakh of India and the Northern areas of Pakistan for a distance of about 550 km. It originates from the Rimo Glacier, one of the tongues of Siachen Glacier. The river widens at the confluence with the Nubra river.

Nubra: The Nubra river is a tributary of the Shyok river and flows in Ladakh region. It originates from the Siachen Glacier.

IMPORTANT LAKES

A number of lakes are found in the state of Jammu & Kashmir. Most of them are of glacial origin. Some of the important lakes of the state are as follows:

Wular: The Wular lake in Kashmir is the largest freshwater lake in India. It is about 16 km long, 9.6 km wide with ill-defined shores. This lake lies in Bandipore district.

Dal: The Dal lake is a beautiful lake near Srinagar. It is 8 km long and 6.4 km wide. It is the floodlung of the Jhelum. The famous Mughal gardens are situated around it. Floating gardens, found in this lake, grow a large variety of vegetables.

Nagin: The Nagin lake is located at a few distance from the Dal lake. Both the lakes are interconnected by a small water channel. Like Dal lake, it also freezes in the winter.

Anchar: The Anchar lake is swampy area. The Sind Nollah enters this lake from one side and flows out from the other. It is about 8 km long and 3 km wide. Ganderbal is a famous township on its north-west bank.

Mansbal: The Mansbal lake is at a distance of 29 km from Srinagar and is situated in Ganderbal district. It is 5 km long and 1 km wide. It is connected with Jhelum by a canal near Sumbal.

Mansar: The Mansar lake, 62 km from Jammu, is over a mile in length and half-a-mile in width. Besides being a popular excursion destination, it is also a holy site, sharing the legend and sanctity of Lake Mansarovar. On its eastern bank lies the shrine of mythological Sheshnag. People take a holy dip in it on festive occasions.

Harwan: The Harwan lake is situated at a distance of 21 km from Srinagar. It is 278 m long, 137 m wide and 18 m deep. This lake is a source of water supply to Srinagar city.

Hokarsar: The Hokarsar lake lies on the Baramulla road about 13 km from Srinagar. It is about 5 km long and 1.5 km wide. Willow trees are grown in abundance around its banks.

Vishno Pad: The Konsurnag or Vishno Pad lake is situated in the Pir Panjal range at a height of 13,124 ft (4,000 m) above sea level to the south of Shopian. It is about 5 km long and 3 km wide and is the source of the river Vishav. It is at a distance of 34 from Shopian.

Gangabal: The Gangabal lake is situated at a height of 11,713 ft (3,570 m) on the peak of Harmukh mountain.

Sheshnag: The Sheshnag lake is situated near Vavjan, enroute to Shri Amarnath cave. It is at a distance of 28 km from Pahalgam.

Neelang: The Neelang lake is situated in tehsil Badgam at a distance of 10 km from Nagam. It is bounded by dense forest.

There are two more lakes: Tarsar and Marsar; lie on the northern slope of the Harmukh mountain. Marsar lake is the origin of the Canal Sharabkul that provides water to the fountains that play in the Mughal Gardens. Marsar lake flows into the Lidar, which is one of the largest tributaries of Jhelum. Sokh and Dokh are two frozen lakes situated at Harmukh mountain. These are said to be two headrops of Parvati — one a warm drop indicating happiness and another a cold one showing grief. The Pangong is a salty lake in Ladakh. It is about 6.4 km long and 3.2 to 6.4 km wide at a height of 4,267 m above sea level. The other lakes of Ladakh are Patlong, Thaled, Longzang, Pangor and Tsimoriri.

IMPORTANT SPRINGS

Kashmir valley abounds in numerous springs of which Verinag (the source of Jhelum), Martand (Anantnag), Achnabal (Anantnag), Kokernag (Anantnag), Chashma shahi (famous for its fresh and digestive water, situated near Srinagar on one side of Boulevard road), Tullamulla or Khirbhawani (a sacred spring), Vicharanag, Sukhnag, Vishnosar and Harmukat Ganga in Srinagar area and Chirnagad Vasaknag in Anantnag are very famous.

The district Kupwara abounds in many famous springs such as Kajinag at Kajinag Mountain, Trehnam Nag at Trehnam town, Ghazinag at Ghazrial Kralapora, Zatishah Nag at Drugmulla, Lolenag at Lalapora Lolab, Shumanag at Trehgam and Mirnag at Haihama Kupwara.

7 Forests

The J & K and Lakakh (UTs) have 22538 sq. km. under forest area constituting about 10.14% of total geographical area of 2,22,236 sq. km. Out of the recorded forest area of 20,230 sq. km., area under reserved forest is 17,643 sq. km, protected forest 2,551 sq. km. and the remaining 36 sq. km. are unclassified. Looking to division wise distribution of forest cover 8128 sq. km. are in Kashmir valley, 12066 sq. km. in Jammu division and 36 sq. km. in Ladakh region constituting 50.97%, 45.89% and 0.06% respectively of the geographical area. Per capita forest area accounts for 0.17 hectares as compared to 0.07 hectares as the national level.

Species-wise forest area reveals 90.68% under coniferous with 5.32% Deodar, 9.02% Chir, 9.73% Kail, 16.81% Fir and 49.80% others. 9.32% forest cover is claimed by non-coniferous non-commercial reserves.

PROTECTED AREA NETWORK (PAN)

The Jammu & Kashmir and Lakakh have 5 National Parks, 16 Sanctuaries, 37 Reserve Area covering an area of about 15,806 sq. km. However, they still has a small proportion of total area under the PAN.

NATIONAL PARKS OF J & K AND LADAKH

Name of National Parks	Area	Region	Key Species
Dachigam	141.00	Kashmir	Hangul/Musk Deer/Brown Bear/Black Bear/Leopard/Kashmiri Flying Squirrel/Otter/Goral
Salim Ali	9.07	Srinagar	Hangu/Serow/Chakar/Monal/Kashmiri antelop
Hemis	3350.00	Ladakh	Ladakh Urial/Tibetan Argali/Blue Sheep/Snow Leopard/Tibetan Wolf/Himalayan Ibex/Himalayan Marmot/Western Kiang/ Brown Bear
Kishtwar	310.00	Jammu	Markhor/Musk Deer/Himalayan Ibex/Snow Leopard/Black Bear
Kazinag	---	---	---

MAJOR KASHMIR SANCTUARIES

Name of Sanctuaries	Area	Region	Key Species
Baltal	203.00	Kashmir	Unavailable
Gulmarg	186.00	Kashmir	Black Bear/Musk Deer/Langoor/ Rhesus Macaque
Hokersar	10.00	Kashmir	Otter/WEP/PFE
Hirapora	11.00	Kashmir	Musk Deer/Kashmir Flying Squirrel/ Himalayan Marmot/Brown Bear/Black Bear
Limber	26.00	Kashmir	Wastern Tragopan/Ladakh Urial/ Goral/Musk Deer/Kashmir Flying Squirrel
Overa	32.00	Kashmir	Leopard/Leopard Cat/Kashmir Flying Squirrel/Brown Bear/Black Bear/Musk Deer/Monal/KLS
Overa-Aru	425.00	Kashmir	Leopard/Leopard Cat/Brown Bear/ Black Beer/Musk Deer/Monal/KLS
Thajwas	203.00	Kashmir	Unavailable
Lachipora	80.00	Kashmir	Western Tragopan/Cheer Pheasant/ Goral/Musk Deer/Ladakh Urial

8 Agriculture

CROPS

Rice: It is the most dominant crop in the entire J&K and Ladakh UTs. It can be well grown in the hot and moist climate as well. Paddy crop (rice) is usually transplanted in the third week of May, while in the external plains of Jammu it is transplanted in the beginning of July, on the commencement of monsoon. The valley of Kashmir, in the state is famous as the "Rice Bowl". The Tehsil of Ranbir Singhpura (Jammu) is famous for its Basmati Rice. Rice is majorly grown in the districts of Jammu, Anantnag, Baramulla, Kupwara, Srinagar, Pulwama and Kathua. The average yield of paddy crop in the Jammu division, per hectare is about 28.3 quintals, while in Kashmir division, it is about 36.5 quintals per hectare.

Wheat: It is the second, major, significant crop in the J&K and Ladakh UTs. It needs cold and moist weather conditions to grow. It also needs 30 cm to 50 cm of rainfall. It is a "Kharif" crop in Ladakh region, while "rabi" crop in Jammu and Kashmir. The fields are ploughed, many-a-time, before sowing the seeds. Wheat is mainly produced in Jammu, Kathua, Udhampur and Rajouri. The total area under production of wheat in the State is about 2,59,000 hectares.

Maize: It is one of the most important cereal crop of the both UTs. It covers around 30 per cent of the total cropped region. It needs warm and moist weather conditions. It is mainly used as food for the people living in Kandi areas. It is also used as a green fodder. Around 30 per cent of the gross cropped area of the state, in 1983-84 was reserved for the cultivation of Maize. The leading maize producing areas of Jammu Division are Rajouri, Doda, Poonch, Udhampur etc. The important areas in the Kashmir Division are Kupwara, Baramulla and Anantnag etc.

Saffron: It is the significant cash crop of Jammu and Kashmir. The Saffron crop needs very different weather conditions to grow. The conditions of extreme cold and extreme heat is not supportive for saffron. Moderate weather conditions with light snowing is ideal for saffron cultivation. This crop is extremely expensive to grow. The labour and seeds costs very high. This is harvested in October and early November. In this period, picking of Saffron flowers just after the disappearance of dew is ideal to get pleasant fragrance. These days Saffron cultivation is being done in various Tehsils of five districts in Kashmir Division.

It is mainly grown in Pulwama Tehsil with 75 per cent of the total saffron production.

Shortcomings' in Agriculture

1. Shortage of advanced and modern resources.
2. Damage to the textural and chemical properties.
3. Depletion of the fertile layers of the soil through soil erosion.
4. Agricultural marketing is very expensive in the state. It becomes costly because of the distance between the fruit gardens' and the markets. The hyped transportation costs makes the fruits very expensive, in terms of competing with fruits of other states.

HORTICULTURE

Jammu & Kashmir is well known for its horticulture produce both in India and abroad. The state offers good scope for cultivation of all types of horticulture crops covering a variety of temperate fruits like apple, pear, peach, plum, apricot, almonds, cherry and sub-tropical fruits like mango, guava, citrus, litchi etc. Apart from this, well known spices like saffron and zeera are cultivated in some parts of the state. Horticulture is emerging as a fast growing sector in the state. Its importance is visualised by its contribution to the state's economy which is estimated to be 7-8%. Almost 45% economic returns in agriculture sector is accounted for by horticulture produce. Seven lakh families comprising 33 lakh people are involved in horticulture trade.

The horticulture department has reported that an area of 3.35 lakh hectares was under horticulture during the year 2011-12 (Nov. 2011) showing an increase of 3.04% over the previous year's area figures. In the area figures highest share of 44.10% is claimed by apple followed by 24.85% walnut.

The production of fruit for the year 2011-12 was reported to be 21.61 lakh tonnes registering an increase of 26.23% over the fruit production figures for 2009-10. Out of total fruit production for 2011-12, 19.32 lakh tonnes constituting 89.84% are fresh fruit and the remaining 10.16% are dry fruit. In the fruit production figures share of apple accounts for 80.84% and walnut with 10.41% share is the next major fruit.

FRUITS

Apple

Amri (Ambri Kashmiri): Lawrence describes it as "the most popular apple in Kashmir .... a sweet fruit ripening in October and keeping its condition for a long time and finding favour with the natives of India for its sweetness and its handsome appearance". Ambri is indigenous to Kashmir and continues to enjoy superiority by virtue of its crisp, sweet flesh and excellent aroma. The fruit is blushed red, striped, medium-sized and oblong to conical in shape with longer storage life. The fruit matures in the last week of September to first week of October. It is an excellent dessert variety.

American trel (American Apirogue) : This variety has crisp juicy, greenish white and sweet flesh and is usually medium-sized, as a result of which it has become very popular with consumers. Oblate-shaped, blushed and patchy red with a smooth surface, it matures in the last week of September. A good dessert variety.

Delicious (Red Delicious): A world-renowned variety. It is one of the most widely grown apples. The fruit is tapering in shape with characteristic five lobes at the apex. Skin is smooth, striped and blushed red. Flesh is fine grained, greenish white, sweet, very juicy and crisp with good aroma. Size is medium to large and it matures by the end of September. A good dessert variety.

Maharaji (White Dotted Red): A large-sized apple with bright red colour on a green base with conspicuous dots. Flesh is crisp, very juicy, acidic and aromatic. The variety sweetens in storage and in an excellent keeper. The fruit matures in late October. It is also a cooking and dessert variety.

Hazaratbali (Benoni): A medium-sized apple with rounds to slightly conical in shape and red to striped skin; white juicy and sweet flesh. It is the earliest variety of apple available from the valley, maturing in mid-July.

Kesri (Cox's Orange Pippin): An old English medium-sized apple; it is round to conical in shape with skin orange red deepening to bright red. The flesh is yellow, firm, crisp, tender and very juicy. A dessert apple with good aroma and sub-acidic taste. The fruit matures in mid August.

Pear

Nakh Kashmiri (Chinese Sandy Pear): This variety gets its name from grained flesh. A conical shaped, small to medium sized variety with crisp, white and juicy flesh. The skin is thick and green in colour that turns yellow on ripening. Carries well in storage and is an excellent dessert variety.

Williams: A widely known English variety. The fruit is large-sized and symmetrical. Skin is yellow with faint blush. The flesh is fine, grained, juicy and sweet. The fruit matures in mid July. A good dessert variety and the choice of canners.

Cherry

Gilas Double (Bigarreau Napoleon): This variety is large-sized anti attractive with cream-red colour. The flesh is firm and juicy but slightly acidic. A good keeper; excellent for canning, and dessert purposes.

Gilas Awal Number (Guigne Pourpera Pecoce): Medium-sized, light red coloured and quite fleshy. The flesh is juicy and sweet with acidic tinge. First to come in the market in May. A good dessert variety.

Gilas Misri (Bigarreau Noir Grossa): Large sized and red coloured; its skin is firm and flesh is sweet and juicy. A good dessert variety.

Walnut

Kashmir walnuts are popular within the country as well as in foreign markets; a source of substantial foreign exchange. On the basis of shell thickness these are grouped as "Burzil". "Kagzi" and "Wont"; corresponding to "Paper-shelled". Walnut Kernels are used in confectionery, as dessert and for extraction of oil.

Almond

Kashmir almonds are known for their superiority of taste and are very popular with the consumers. Like walnuts these are also grouped on the basis of shell thickness as "Papery", "Thin-shelled", and "Thick-shelled". Considered as highly nourishing and of great medicinal value, its kernels are used in confectionery as well as dessert. Its trees are the first blooming fruit trees and an enchanting sight that lends glamour to the spring in Kashmir.

Peaches

Quetta: Fruit medium to above medium, pointed, halves acuminate. Skin thick, downy, Yellow base with scattered red patches. Flesh firm, creamy yellow, moderately juicy, sweet with acidic blend when fully ripe. Free stone. The fruit is ready for harvest in 3rd week of August.

Apricot

Gilgati Sweet: Fruit medium, from oblong to rather ovate, slightly irregular in shape. Cavity rather deep to medium in depth, regular and acute. Skin yellow when fresh (brown yellow when dried) sweet, moderately flavoured, stone free kernel sweet. Ready for picking in the last week of June.

Strawberry

Strawberry is earliest fruit available in Srinagar market during April. Sub-tropical areas in Jammu have potential to grow the crop under irrigated condition. It is valued for easy propagation, early maturity, high yield with 5 to 9 per cent sugar. Plants start bearing in second year. Over 2000 varieties of garden strawberry are known with large fruit, weighing 30-70 grams.

Plums

Santa Rosa: Fruit medium, roundish, regular, skin smooth and thin flesh deep red, juicy, sweet and soft full of aroma, stone cling type.

FLORICULTURE

Floriculture sector has been identified as the most focussed segment of horticulture. There is much more income to farmers from flower cultivation due to growing demand for flowers in domestic and foreign markets. To promote this segment floriculture nurseries have been developed where ornamental and medicinal plants are produced, besides the seed multiplication programmes of flower seeds. The Directorate of Floriculture produces more than 40 lakh seedlings of different kinds of flowers and ornamental plants not only for its own requirement but also sells the seedlings to the flower lovers on cash payment and earns revenue of Rs. 8 lakh on this account per annum. One of the landmark achievement of floriculture department has been the establishment of Tulip Garden first of its kind of Siraj Bagh Srinagar. Situated on the foothills of the mighty Zabarwan mountains the garden has the distinction of being Asia's largest Tulip garden. The garden remains in full bloom for one month (last week of March to last week of April). The garden witness highest inflow of tourists which includes film making companies for shooting song sequences in this beautiful garden.

FLOWERS

Flower Kerria Japonica: Deciduous, arching, graceful shrub butter cup like, golden yellow flowers are borne along green shoots. From mid to late spring, foliage is bright green.

Flower Visteria: Deciduous, woody-stemmed, twining climber leaflets, scented, pea like violet flowers are carried in Drooping recemes blooms in early spring.

Flower Tulip: Tulips are excellent in the rock Gardens informal bedding, as elegant cut flowers and for containers. A large variety of the hybrids are now available. Flowers mid spring, propagation by bulbs.

Flower Magnolia Liliflora: Deciduous shrub with open habit oval to pear shaped, dark green leaves, large deep purple, flowers, creamy white flushed purple inside.

Flower Chaen-Omelee Speciose: Well branched, spreading shrub dark green glossy leaves and bowl shaped flower about 5 cm. across from mid winter to mid spring small to medium, propagation by cutting seeds and layering.

9 Irrigation

In Jammu & Kashmir and Ladakh the total net area irrigated by different sources (canals, tanks, wells and others) was about 2.61 lakh hectare (41.96 per cent) in the year 1950-51. In 2015-16 the area under this category was 4.37 lakh hectare.

The J & K and Ladakh can be divided into 3 hydro-geological units, namely, (i) Outer plains of Jammu & Kathua districts (ii) Kashmir Valley and (iii) Ladakh region.

Outer Plains of Jammu & Kathua Districts

The outer plain unit is located at the foothills of Shivalik Hills. The altitude varies between 260 and 440 metres above mean sea level. Innumerable streams are crossing the area. These streams are locally called *khads* and are laid by boulders and have water only in the rainy season. These plains are further divided into Bhabar and Tarai region. Because of deeper water level conditions, the Bhabar region has ground water only in under-water level condition, whereas in the Tarai region it occurs both in under-water level and confined conditions. Jammu area receives surface irrigation facilities from the following canal systems:

1. The Ranbir canal system
2. Partap canal system
3. The Kashmir canal system
4. The High canal system
5. The Ravi-Tawi irrigation system.

About 90 per cent of the above-surface irrigation facilities are available to the Tarai area and only 10 per cent to the Bhabar area. There is considerable scope for extending irrigation facilities through tubewells in the Bhabar area, which has not so far been covered by surface irrigation.

Kashmir Valley

Kashmir valley hydro-geological unit located at an elevation of 1600-1900 metres above mean sea level with its trend in NW-SE direction. The Pir Panjal range along south and southwest and Great Himalayan range of the north and northeast encircle this valley. It seems that inland independent ground water

33

region of the valley is plain. A Karewas level land is a conspicuous feature of the valley. There are several hard rock ridges, which abut into the valley plain from the flanks and are responsible for marking almost separate hydro-geological sub basins. Lowlying areas, especially those around the surface water bodies are marshy. The Dal, the Wular and the Manasbal lakes occupy about 300 sq.km of the valley portion. The lakes act as balancing reservoir for storing flood water and save downstream areas from watercourse.

Ladakh Region

The third one is the Ladakh region. The sediments of Leh plain consist of morainic material overlain by varied living and silts of lacustrine. The entire zone receives irrigated water for cultivation from the Indus and its tributaries as well as Nallah, Drass, Suru, Kangi and Wakha. In this region the construction of tubewells is possible on the thickness of rocks.

AREA IRRIGATED FROM DIFFERENT SOURCES

The net area sown in the J & K and Ladakh during 2012-13 was 744 thousand hectares whereas the gross area sown (total area sown under different crops) was 1162 thousand hectares. The mode of irrigating the crops mainly used is the canals. About 88 per cent of the net area irrigated is irrigated through canals while tanks, tube wells and other means are also used. The net area irrigated through different means for the years 2010-11 to 2012-13 is given in the following table:

Area Irrigated (thousand hectares) by Source

Source	Net Area Irrigated		
	2010-11	**2011-12**	**2012-13**
Canals	288.48	285.40	285.35
	(91.88%)	(89.40%)	(87.78%)
Tanks	5.02	7.10	8.02
	(1.60%)	(2.22%)	(2.47%)
Wells	6.21	7.42	10.42
	(1.98%)	(2.32%)	(3.20%)
Other sources	14.28	19.33	21.29
	(4.54%)	(6.06%)	(6.55%)
Total	**313.99**	**319.26**	**325.08**

A slight increase was witnessed, during the year 2012-13, in the net area irrigated, as it increased from 319.26 thousand hectares in 2011-12 to 325.08 thousand hectares. However, when net area irrigated for the year 2012-13 is compared with the figures for 1974-75, one observes an increase of only 30 thousand hectares in the irrigation potential utilized over a period of more than three decades.

The inter district position shows that the net as well as gross sown area in Leh and Kargil are cent per cent irrigated. Among the districts with large Gross Area Irrigated, Ganderbal has 77.15 per cent, Anantnag has 73.20 per cent, and Shopian has 72.98 per cent. Districts with very low percentage of gross area irrigated are Reasi (6.56%), Ramban (7.34%). The District-wise details of Gross Area Sown and Gross Area Irrigated for the year 2012-13 are as follows:

Gross Area Irrigated as Percentage of Gross Area Sown

S. No.	District/ Region	Gross area sown (Ha)	Gross area irrigated (Ha)	Gross area irrigated as %age of gross area sown
		2012-13	2012-13	2012-13
1.	Srinagar	10230	7365	71.99
2.	Ganderbal	18691	14420	77.15
3.	Shopian	25207	18397	72.98
4.	Anantnag	71432	52288	73.20
5.	Kulgam	39312	27397	69.69
6.	Pulwama	57564	38345	66.61
7.	Budgam	55734	37551	67.38
8.	Jammu	187717	110847	59.05
9.	Bandipora	24017	13175	54.86
10.	Kupwara	49581	26698	53.85
11.	Baramulla	65734	30063	45.73
12.	Kathua	122575	40615	33.13
13.	Samba	60610	15037	24.81
14.	Poonch	45310	6551	14.46
15.	Kishtwar	23465	3359	14.31
16.	Doda	39541	3799	9.61
17.	Rajouri	99161	8632	8.71
18.	Reasi	40854	2679	6.56
19.	Ramban	24943	1830	7.34
20.	Udhampur	82135	10131	12.33
21.	Kargil	10914	10914	100.00
22.	Leh	7367	7367	100.00

Crops Irrigated

The crops which are provided irrigation are rice, wheat, maize, oil seeds and fruits & vegetables. Among these crops, rice, which needs to be kept covered with shallow water, claimed maximum percentage of area under irrigation. In fact, around 90% of the area irrigated was under rice in 2012-13. 28% area under wheat and 9.37% under maize was also irrigated during the same year.

Strategy for the 12th Five Year Plan

1. Focus on completion of ongoing projects to avoid cost and time over runs.

2. Bridging the gap between potential created and potential utilized through command areas Development Programmes and activating the water user Associations.

3. Increasing water use efficiency by proper maintenance of canal and distributor network, addressing damage of lining in lined canals, collapse of slopes, leakages in gates, filed channels etc.

4. Creation of awareness and sensitization of farmers.

5. Building capacities of Engineers to move from a narrow construction-orientation to management roles as well.

6. Selective new projects for those areas where irrigation infrastructure is underdeveloped or need to be addressed for exploring irrigation potential in big way.

7. Comprehensive programme for mapping aquifers and strong partnerships and coordination between Govt. departments, Research Institutes, PRI's, Civil Society organisations, local communities etc.

8. Properly Maintenance of water bodies.

❑ ❑ ❑

10 Power

Electricity is an essential source of commercial energy which is vital for sustained Economic Growth. The increase in demand for power means the economy is growing and is leading to modernization, industrialization and improvement in basic amenities culminating into a better quality of life of the people.

Jammu & Kashmir and Ladakh UTs are bestowed with significant hydel potential which when exploited fully will provide a strong impetus for the growth of the State's economy. The development of this potential would need huge resources, technical expertise, administrative reforms, congenial environment, proper regulation and management, besides competitive marketing, Policy formation and private participation. The optimal exploitation of the available hydel resources in the both UTs would not only meet the State's demand but will also supply power to the Northern grid to boost the overall development of the State.

The estimated hydro power potential of the J&K and Ladakh is 20,000 Megawatts (MW), of which about 16480 MW have been identified. Out of the identified potential, only 2693.45 MW. 16% (of identified potential) has been exploited so far, consisting of 761.96 MW in State Sector from 21 power projects, 1889 MW from seven power projects under Central Sector, i.e., 690 MW Salal Hydel Electric Project, 480 MW Uri-I Hydel Electric Project, 390 MW Dulhasti, 120 MW Sewa-II, 45 MW Nimo Bazgo, 44 MW Chutak and 240 MW Uri-II (2 units of 120 MW commissioned) and 42.5 MW from two private sector projects. The installed capacity of 761.96 MW from state sector projects includes the 450 MW of Baghlihar Phase–I constructed at a cost of ₹ 5827 crores by the J&K State Power Development Corporation which was commissioned on 9-10-2008. This State of the Art project is located on Chenab basin at Chanderkote in district Ramban.

Recognizing the need of development of this sector, the both UTs has started giving due importance to this sector. In this backdrop, during the 10th Five Year Plan, many initiatives were taken which included setting up of Power Development Corporation & State Electricity Regulatory Commission, identification of power potential, involvement of private participation, Joint Ventures, sanctioning of projects, signing of tripartite MoU between Ministry of

Finance, Planning Commission and Government of Jammu and Kashmir in 2006, special support from Central Government under PM's Reconstruction Plan, State plan as well as other Centrally Sponsored Schemes in the Power Sector for generation, modernization, up gradation and efficient transmission of the power.

Prime Minister's Re-construction Plan (PMRP)

To meet the gap of infrastructure at 220 kV and 132 kV level, various schemes have been taken up under Prime Minister's Reconstruction Programme at a cost of ₹ 1351.00 Crores. Cumulative expenditure under the scheme ending 2012-13 is of the order of ₹ 1111.98 crores which includes 18.26 crores for laying of fibre optic communication system which have been advanced to PGCIL. PGCIL has awarded the project to TCIL.

Rajiv Gandhi Grameen Vidyutikaran Yojana (RGGVY, Phase-I)

RGGVY is basically a scheme for 100% Rural Electrification. 14 Schemes covering whole of J&K and Ladakh UTs were submitted to REC at a total estimated DPR (Detailed Project Report) cost of ₹ 1051.73 crores. All these schemes have been sanctioned by REC at a cost of ₹ 940.06 crores and ₹ 797.71 crores have been released ending 06/2013.

RGGVY Phase-II

Objective of RGGVY Phase-II scheme.

- Electrifying all villages and habitations as per new definition.
- Providing access to electricity to all rural households.
- Providing electricity connection to Below Poverty Line (BPL) families free of charge.

Per Capita Consumption

Per capita consumption in J&K and Ladakh UTs has shown steady growth and presently it is around 928 units against national average of around 900 units for the year 2012-13. Due to extreme climatic conditions in most parts of the both UTs the per capita consumption is low. The issue needs to be addressed by increased generation for which the state has framed ambitious plans to add 9000 MW during 12th and 13th Plan period.

Rural Electrification Programme

Rural electrification programme in J&K and Ladakh has been followed up quite vigorously as in the other states of the country. The total number of villages/ hamlets electrified till date rose to 20203 (6554 villages+13649 hamlets). Under RGGVY schemes 283 unelectrified/de-electrified villages are targeted to be electrified out of which 192 villages stand electrified as on October-2013.

HYDEL POLICY 2011

State Government approved Hydel Policy 2011 for development of small projects (2-100 MW) in the State through IPP mode on BOOT basis. The main features are:

- Projects upto 10 MW reserved for state subjects with relaxed technical criteria.
- 15% free power + 1% LADF to be provided to State
- Projects to be allotted on BOOT basis to be returned to State after 35 years.
- Upfront Premiums ranging from 4.0 lacs to 8.0 lacs / MW as per the capacity of the projects.
- Tariff based bidding for project above 25 MWs.
- Terminal value for return of project to be not more than 10% of the cost of the project at the time of bidding.
- 30% power (excluding 15% free power + 1% LADF) to be procured by the State with first right refusal for remaining power.
- Allotment of project through transparent competitive bidding.
- PDC Nodal Agency for Land acquisition, IWT clearance, Forest clearance etc.
- Incentive by way of non imposition of water usage charges for Ist ten years, exemption from Entry Tax / Income Tax available to IPPs, besides incentive available from MNRE, GoI.
- Model Implementation Agreement and PPA integral part of the reserved Hydel Policy 2011. Timelines / mile stone fixed as part of the agreement.

RENEWABLE ENERGY

The Science & Technology Department through its Agency (Jammu & Kashmir Energy Development Agency - JAKEDA) continue with its concerted efforts to improve the power scenario in the State, the utilization of new and renewable sources of energy to supplement the power requirement, with focus on un-electrified villages, hamlets, remote and inaccessible areas, would receive priority. Jammu and Kashmir Energy Development Agency (JAKEDA) is a state Nodal Agency working under the administrative control of the Science and Technology Department J&K Government for the promotion and implementation of projects aimed at meeting the energy requirements in general and un-electrified areas of the state in particular by harnessing new and renewable sources of energy such as: 1. Solar Energy, 2. Wind energy, 3. Small hydro power (up to 2 MW), 4. Bio-Energy (Bio-Biomass/Bio-wastes/Agricultural/Rural/Urban/Industrial), 5. New energy sources (Hydrogen, geothermal, Tidal, etc)

 # Transportation & Communication

In the landlocked state like Jammu and Kashmir, road transport is an indispensable means of communication for the regular distribution of essential and other commodities. The government has given the highest priority to the construction and maintenance of roads.

RAILWAYS

The state was brought on the Railway map of India in 1970 when the city of Jammu-Tawi was connected with Pathankot with rail. The total length of railway lines in the state was about 80 km at that time. The railway line between Jammu and Udhampur was completed by 1997-98. ₹ 192 crores have been spent on its completion and 53 km rail link was completed in April 2005. The extension of this railway line upto Srinagar was planned at an additional cost of ₹ 1900 crores. Udhampur-Katra and Banihal-Baramulla rail link projects have been taken up as a national project in 2002. The 287 km rail line, connecting Udhampur-Srinagar-Baramulla, is vital for Jammu and Kashmir for its socio-economic development, promoting national integration and strengthening infrastructure of the state.

This project is divided into four sections:

I. 53 km stretch from Jammu to Udhampur which stand completed in April 2005.

II. 25 Km stretch from Udhampur to Katra which is completed in May 2014.

III. Stretch of 116 km from Katra to Banihal is in process under Konkan Railway Corporation Ltd.

IV. Stretch 132 km from Banihal to Baramulla is also in operation.

ROADS

The J&K and Ladakh UTs are connected to the rest of the country through just one highway (NH 1A), 400 kms stretch (approx) maintained by Border Roads Organization (BRO) of India. As Railway network of the State is in infancy stage, this has rendered the State totally dependent on road connectivity which provides links to the remote areas of the State.

Central Road Fund

Central Road Fund is a flagship programme which is primarily focussed for development of State Roads including Roads of Inter State Connectivity and

Economic Importance. Although Central Road Fund is a National Flagship Scheme is part of the State Plan and funding is made by the Govt. of India as ACA to the State Plan. 100 schemes stand sanctioned since the inception of the Programme in 2000-01, out of which 64 schemes have been completed ending November, 2013.

Flagship Programme—PMGSY

The Pradhan Mantri Gram Sadak Yojana (PMGSY) is a flagship programme which was launched in December, 2000 in the country and also extended to J&K State in the same year. The objective of the PMGSY programme is to provide connectivity by way of all weather roads to the unconnected habitations in rural areas. Under Bharat Nirman Programme, it is envisaged to provide road connectivity to all the unconnected habitations in the country having population more than 1000 souls as per census 2001 whereas in hilly states and desert areas the target is to provide connectivity with population size of 500 souls and above.

Presently, 2038 schemes at an estimated cost of ₹ 5486.14 crore have been sanctioned under this programme in nine phases, against which an amount of ₹ 2462.94 crore stands released by GOI ending November, 2013 against which ₹ 2382.86 crore stands utilized. So far 891 schemes have been completed. A total road length of 4968 kms have also been completed till date.

Four Lanning of National Highway

The 4-lanning of National Highway 396 kms from Lakhanpur to Srinagar is being executed by National Highway Authority of India at an estimated cost of ₹ 592.47 Crore as part of North South Corridor under National Highway Development Project (NHDP) Phase II. 115 kms have been already completed in six packages in Phase I.

The Phase II of Srinagar-Jammu section is in progress. In respect of Panthachowk Quazigund, the progress is 24% and in case of Quazigund–Banihal tunnel, the progress is 22.15%. In respect of the Chenani Nashri tunnel, progress has improved to 44.50%. In respect of Udhampur Sidhra, it has improved to 71%.

MAIN ROADS

1. **Srinagar—Shopian Road:** 95 kms long. Sopore connected with Teethwal through Handwara, Trehgem and Chowhibal.
2. **Jhelum Valley Road:** 133 kms long road. It connects Srinagar with Baramulla and Uri. It is a National Highway.
3. **Dhar—Udhampur Road:** A defence Road is connecting Dhar with Udhampur.
4. **Jammu—Pathankot Road:** It is the National highway, 108 kms long. It links the state with rest of the country.
5. **Banihal Cart Road:** 300 kms long, connectivity for Jammu and Kashmir. Connectivities of the road connect other areas among themselves.

6. **Jammu—Poonch Road:** 230 kms long Important from Defence point of view.

7. **Srinagar—Shopian Road:** It is 53 kms long and branches off from Pampore.

8. **Srinagar—Baltal Road:** 118 kms long, passes through Ganderbal and crosses through Sindh Nullah.

9. **Srinagar—Wayil Road:** Road passes through Achhabal, Kokarnag and is 85 kms long.

10. **Batote, Doda, Bhadherwah and Kishtwar Road:** Doda and Kishtwar connected Doda is 45 kms from Batote, Bhadherwah 53 kms and away from Doda.

11. **Srinagar—Pahalgam Road:** 98 kms long, passes through Anantnag and Mattan from Pahalgam. It leads to Amarnath cave.

12. **Srinagar—Bandipur Road:** 56 km long leads to Bandipur from Srinagar. It passes through Sumbal, Mansar lake, Safapur and Ajas. From Bandipur, there is a 33 kms long road to Sopore and one to Gurez.

13. **Srinagar Gulmarg Road:** It is 29 kms long, connectivity between Srinagar and Tangmarg and Gulmarg, a tourist place.

AVIATION

There are three major airports in the Jammu & Kashmir and Ladakh UTs providing aerial transport among both UTs and the Country. Out of the three Srinagar airport has been upgraded as international airport named as Sheikh-ul-Alam Airport, while as the facilities at Jammu and Leh airports are also being upgraded. One more airport at Kargil headquarters is connected by Dakota service. Commissioning of Sheikh-ul-Alam International Airport at Srinagar has opened the new vistas for enhancing connectivity at International level which will inturn facilitate international tourism, promote international trade especially export which will provide a big push to the economy and generate avenues of better employment.

COMMUNICATION

Communication facilities have considerably expanded with the opening of new telephone exchanges, extension of existing lines and the establishment of direct-dialing services between Srinagar and Jammu, Srinagar and Delhi and between Srinagar, Anantnag and Baramulla. This service has been extended upto Mumbai and other important towns in the country. The much awaited mobile telephony was launched in Jammu & Kashmir by BSNL in August 2003. A new radio transmitter of much greater power has since been installed in Jammu, and the Srinagar station has been further strengthened. A radio station has since been set up in Leh. The TV station in Srinagar, catering to a population of more than 20 lakhs, has become very popular. Similar is the case with the Jammu TV station.

❏ ❏ ❏

◆12▶ Minerals

COAL

(*i*) **Occurrance :** The coal is extracted from Kalakot coal fields which extends from Jangalgali in the cast to Jigni in the West, falling in Districts of Udhampur and Rajouri and lies between latitude 30°-15° to 33°-15° and Longitude 74°-20° and 75°-10°.

This coal which is semi anthracitic in rank occurs as black in form though about 10% of the production is in the form of Steam coal. The coal is of generally of high heat value.

(*ii*) **Uses:** This coal is used in

(*a*) Manufacture of cement using V.S.K. Technology.

(*b*) Brick Kiln Industry.

(*c*) Steam coal is used in Industries using boilers.

(*d*) In manufacture of battery covers.

GYPSUM

(*i*) **Occurrance :** The Gypsum deposits occur in Buniyar in Distt. Baramullah and in areas of Ramban and Assar in Distt. Doda of J&K State. J&K Minerals Limited is actively mining Gypsum from Assar Gypsum mine which is situated at 30 K.M. from Batote on N.H.-IS and is envisaging to expoit huge gypsum reserves from Parianka area in Ramban. The Gypsum so mined is of purity of 97% and is in form of lumps.

(*ii*) **Uses:** Gyspum is used in.

(*a*) Making of plaster of paris.

(*b*) Manufacture of cement.

(*c*) Manufacture of Gypsum Boards.

(*d*) Land Reconditioning

(*e*) Pharmaceutical Industry

(*f*) Black Board Chalk

(*g*) Ceramics Industry for Pottery Moulds.

SAPPHIRE

- (*i*) **Occurance** : The Sapphire occurs in Paddar area in Distt. Doda, J&K State, which lies between longitude of 76 Deg.-15 Deg. and 76 Deg. -30 Deg. at a height of 4500 m above M.S.L.
- (*ii*) **Quality:** The Sapphire of paddar is deep bluish in colour and is world renowned Gem-stone for its clarity and transparency.

  Uses: Mainly used in Jewellery and has a high ornamental value.

MAGNESITE

- (*i*) **Occurance** : The Chipprian Magnesite deposit is located 3 KM away from Panthal village in Udhampur Distt. J&K State. Panthal village is situated 15 KM from Tikri (NH-IA) on Tikri-Katra Route. The deposits are located in rugged, hi lly topography at an altitude of 1481 Mts. SML.

  This deposit is worked in a Joint venture between M/s JKML and JK Minerals Development Corporation. The Magnasite is of high grade and it is proposed to feed the magnesite arc after crushing to proper size Rotary kilns from Obtaining dead burnt magnesite.

- (*ii*) **Uses:**
  - (*a*) The dead burnt Magnasite is used in manufacture of Refractory Bricks.
  - (*b*) Magnasite is used in Medicines and Cosmetics.

LIME STONE

- (*i*) **Occurance** : High grade lime-stone both cement grade and chemical grade occur in a abundance in Distt, of Anantnag, Pulwama and Baramulla Distt of J&K State.

  J&K minerals is exploiting cement grade lime stone at Khrew in Distt. Pulwama.

- (*ii*) **Uses:** The Lime stone is used in manufacturer of cement and lime.

LIGNITE

- (*i*) **Occurance** : The lignite deposits occur in Nichohama 50 KM from Srinagar in Distt. Kupwara, J&K. The detailed exploration has been carried out by GSI and Mineral exploration Corporation Limited and more than 5 Million tonnes of Deposits have been proved.

  J&K mineral is envisaging to exploit this deposit as captive product for Thermal Power Station to be set up at site.

PCC PRODUCTS

J&K Minerals has its two units of Precast Cement products at Muyan (Kashmir) and Bari-Brahmana (Jammu). The main products manufactured are.

(*i*) PCC Poles 7.5,8.0 and 9.0 Meters in length.

(*ii*) Spun Pipes of sizes.

NP-2 and NP-3 classes, 3 size varying from 100 m dia to 1200 mm dia.

(*iii*) Terrazo Tiles.

(*iv*) Hollow Blocks.

Uses:

(*a*) PCC Poles are generally used in Power Transmission Lines.

(*b*) Spun Pipes are used in Civil works i.e. Sewerage, Culverts and for water supply.

(*c*) Terrazo Tiles are used for ornamental flooring.

MARBLE

(*i*) **Occurance** : Marble deposits occur in Kupwara, Kashmir in various hues and colours. J&K Minerals is exploiting marble at Drug-Mulla, Kupwara.

(*ii*) **Uses** : The Marble Salbs after cutting, polishing and finishing are used in flooring, walling and as stable tops.

❑ ❑ ❑

13 ▸ Education

In Jammu & Kashmir and Ladakh education is free up to university stage. Seasonal schools have been opened for people in the hilly areas and for the scheduled castes.

Yet the both UTs are educationally backward. Against the national literacy rate of 73% the state has a literacy figure of 67.17%. Literacy rate among male is 76.75% and that of female is 56.43% (all figures 2011 census).

On the technical education side, there is one National Institute of Technology (NIT) at Srinagar and one engineering college at Jammu. In addition, there are about nine polytechnics to impart vocational training. District institutes of education have been opened in all the districts of the both UTs to provide extensive and intensive training to the teachers.

The number of colleges providing education in 1950-51 was just 07 including 01 women College. By the year 2015-16, the number of colleges has increased to 95 including 12 women colleges. Moreover, there are 02 State Universities and 05 Government-aided Universities. 15 Off-sites Campuses of the two State Universities have also been sanctioned out of which 09 campuses have already been made functional.

The both UTs has made considerable progress in the field of medical education. There are two medical colleges under University of Kashmir at Srinagar and two under University of Jammu at Jammu. A full-fledged medical institute, Sher-i-Kashmir Medical Institute, is functioning at Bemina, Srinagar. The institute has more than 600-bed complement and provides facilities for post-graduate medical education and medical research.

DISTRICTWISE LITERACY RATE - 2011

District	Persons	Males	Females	District	Persons	Males	Females
Anantnag	62.7	72.7	52.2	Kupwara	64.5	75.7	50.9
Badgam	56.1	66.3	44.8	Leh (Ladakh)	77.2	86.3	63.6
Bandipore	56.3	66.9	44.3	Pulwama	63.5	74.4	51.8
Baramula	64.6	75.5	52.4	Punch	66.7	78.8	53.2
Doda	64.7	78.4	49.7	Rajouri	68.2	78.1	56.6
Ganderbal	58	68.9	45.7	Ramban	54.3	68.8	38
Jammu	83.5	89.1	77.1	Reasi	58.2	68.4	46.6
Kargil	71.3	83.2	56.3	Samba	81.4	88.4	73.6
Kathua	73.1	81.5	63.7	Shupiyan	60.8	70.3	50.9
Kishtwar	56.2	68.9	42.4	Srinagar	69.4	76.2	61.8
Kulgam	59.2	69.6	48.5	Udhampur	68.5	78.4	57.1

# Administration

The earliest administrative unit in the State of Jammu and Kashmir was known as "PARGANA". It was during the Dogra regime that the PARGANAS were reorganized and named as Zilas and Tehsils. The Zilas were further re-designated as Wazarats. In 1892, on the recommendation of Sir Walter Lawrence, there were some re-adjustments in the Wazarats. Consequent upon loss of huge territory of the State to Pakistan in 1947, the Wazarats were reorganized in 1951. Simultaneously the nomenclature of Wazarats was also changed and re-designated as Districts. For administrative convenience the Districts were sub divided into Tehsils and Niabats. Jammu and Kashmir (UT) has 20 districts and Ladakh (UT) has 2 districts. The districts are:

Kashmir Division

1. Anantnag	2. Baramulla	3. Budgam	4. Srinagar
5. Pulwama	6. Kupwara	7. Badipora	8. Ganderbal
9. Kulgam	10. Shopian		

Jammu Division

1. Jammu	2. Kathua	3. Doda	4. Rajouri
5. Poonch	6. Udhampur	7. Kishtwar	8. Ramban
9. Reasi	10. Samba		

ANANTNAG

At a Glance

Educational Institutions	1180	**Tehsil**	6
Health Institutions	271	**Towns**	11
Roads	1265 km	**Blocks**	7
Households	0.98 lakhs	**Panchayats**	297
Area	2,917 sq. km	**Gross Area irrigated**	0.67 lakh hectares
Population	10,78,692 (2011)	**Forests**	1438 sq. km
Population Density	306 persons per sq. km	**Literacy rate**	62.7%
		Bank Branches	78
Villages	393 (19 inhabited)		

Tourist Places: Pahalgam, Kokernag, Acchabal, Verinag and Daksum.

BARAMULLA

At a Glance

Educational Institutions	1275	Towns	7
Health Institutions	368	Blocks	12
Roads	1500 km	Panchayats	365
Area	4,190 sq. km	Gross Area sown	0.91 lakhs hectares
Population	10,08,039 (2011)	Net Area irrigated	0.44 lakhs hectares
Population Density	240 per sq. km	Forests	2963 sq. km
Villages	531	Villages electrified	633
Tehsil	8	Literacy rate	64.6%
		Post Offices	236

Tourist Places: Gulmarg, Watlab, Kishan Ganag, Sopore, etc.

BUDGAM

At a Glance

Educational Institutions	1430	Towns	5
Health Institutions	176(1995-96)	Panchayats	283
Roads	1371 km	C.D. Blocks	8
Area	1371 sq. km	Net Area irrigated	35,000 hectare
Population	7,53,745 (2011)	Villages electrified	492
Population Density	544 per sq. km	Bank Branches	32
Villages	496	Notified Area Committees	5
Tehsil	6	Literacy Rate	56.1%

Historical Places: Tomb of Sheikh Noor-ud-din-Noorani, The Shrine of Khan Saheb, Imam Bara Budgam, Ziarat Alamdar-E-Kashmir, The Tomb of Sham Ded.

Tourist Places: Nilnag, Yusmarg, Sange-safed, Mount Tutakuti and Tosaimaidan etc.

DODA

At a Glance

Educational Institutions	1493	Tehsil	6
Health Institutions	256	Panchayats	231
Area	2985 sq. km	Blocks	8
Population	4,09,936 (2011)	Literacy rate	64.7%
Population Density	46 per sq. km	Bank Branches	52
Villages	405	Post Offices	43

Tourist Places: Bhaderwah, Chinta Valley, Khani Top, Patnitop, Sanasar, Sarthal, Machail, etc.

JAMMU

At a Glance

Educational Institutions	2546	Area	2336 sq. km
Health Institutions	332	Population	15,29,958(2011)
Roads	1609.51 km	Population Density	596 per sq. km
Languages spoken	Dogri, Hindi, Urdu	Villages	859

Tehsil	4	Literacy rate	83.5%
Towns	13	Bank Branches	188
Panchayats	296	Post Offices	223
Blocks	8		

Historical Places: Bahu Fort, Mubarak Mandi Complex, Rani Charak Mahal, Amar Mahal Museum, Ziarat Baba Buddan Shah, Ziarat baba Roshan Shah Wali, Ziarat Peer Mitha, Paanch Peer, Dargah Garib Shah, Peer Khoh, Aap Shambhu Temple Sathrian, Raghunath Temple, Gadhadhariji Temple, Ranbireshwar Temple, Panchbakhter temple, Gurudwara Sh. Guru Nanak Devji, Samadhi Maharani Chand Kour.

Tourist Places: Jhajjar Kotli, Bagh-e-Bahu, Jhiri, Surinsar and Mansar Lakes.

KATHUA

At a Glance

Educational Institutions	948	Panchayats	244
Health Institutions	361	Blocks	8
Road length	784 km	Gross Area irrigated	32,752 hectare
Industrial Units Registered	3476	Villages electrified	548
Area	2,502 sq. km	Literacy rate	73.1%
Population	6,16,435 (2011)		
Population Density	246 per sq. km	Bank Branches	60
Villages	587	Principal Crop	Wheat, Rice, Maize
Tehsil	5	Post Offices	129

Historical Places: Jasrota, Billawar, Mankote, Lakhanpur, Bhadu, Tirikote.
Tourist Places: Basholi, Sarthal, Bani, Billwar, Ujh, Banjal, Sukarala Mata, Peer Fazal Shah, Dhar Mahanpur and Banjal etc.

KUPWARA

At a Glance

Educational Institutions	792	Blocks	11
Health Institutions	222	Gross Area sown	45000 hectare
Area	2379 sq km	Net Area irrigated	23000 hectare
Population	8,70,354 (2011)	Forests	1500 sq. km
Population Density	368 per sq. km	Villages electrified	337
Villages	364	Literacy rate	64.5%
Tehsil	3	Bank Branches	58
Panchayats	356	Post Offices	213

Historical Places: Muqam-e-Shahwali - Mazar-e-sharief of Zattishah, Ziarat -i- Baba Abdullah Gazi, Shrine of Prakash Akhoon, Kheer Bhawani Asthapan.

Tourist Places: Famous Springs, Kajinag - Located at Kajinag Mountain, Trehgam Nag - Trehgam Town, Ghazinag - Ghazrial kralapora, ZatishahNag - Drugmulla, Lolenag - Lalpora Lolab, Shumanag - Trehgam, Mirnag - Caves of Raja Ram, Asmala slope, Tumar Pass, Farktan, Jar Pass, Harwan Pass.

PULWAMA

At a Glance

Educational institutions	756	Tehsil	4
Health Institutions	189	Town area Committees	6
Road length	810 km	Blocks	5
Area	1086 sq. km	Forests	1011 sq. km
Population	5,60,440 (2011)	Villages electrified	551
Population Density	516 per sq. km	Literacy rate	63.5%
Villages	331	Panchayats	186

Historical Places: The Avantishwar Temple, The Payer Temple, Asar Sharief Pintoora, The shrine of Shah Hamdan, Jama Masjid Shopian.

Tourist Places : Aharbal, Nagberan, Shikargah, Tarsar Marsar, Kungwattan and Hurpora, etc.

POONCH

At a Glance

Educational Institutions	779	Panchayats	189
Health Institutions	120	Blocks	6
Area	1,674 sq. km	Literacy rate	66.7%
Population	4,76,835 (2011)	Bank Branches	24
Population Density	285 per sq. km	Principal Crop	Maize, paddy
Villages	179		and wheat
	(168 inhabited)	Post Offices	62
Tehsil	4		

Historical Places: Buddha Amarnath, Ramkund, Ziarat Sain, Nangali Sahib, Ziarat Chhotay Sahib.

Tourist Places: There are several beautiful spots on the foothill of Pir Panchal mountain range. These are: Noori Chamb, Buffliaz, Loran, Behramgata, Girgen, Poonch Fort and Krishna Ghati etc.

UDHAMPUR

At a Glance

Educational institutions	1207	Towns	6
Road length	1094 km	Panchayats	204
Industrial Units Registered	2500	Blocks	7
Area	2473 sq. km	Gross Area sown	71,000 hectare
Population	5,54,985 (2011)	Forests	1920 sq. km
Population Density	211 per sq. km	Literacy rate	68.5%
Villages	357	Bank Branches	50
Tehsil	4	Principal Crop	Maize

Historical Places: Babore Temples, Krimchi Temples, Sri Mata Vaishno Devi Shrine, Sheesh Mahal of Ramnagar, Ramnagar Fort, Ghora Gali.

Tourist Places: Patnitop-Mantalai, Latti, Sansar and Naka Seoj Dhar

RAJOURI

At a Glance

Educational Institutions	955	Panchayats	295
Health Institutions	193 (including ISM)	Blocks	8
Area	2,630 sq. km	Gross Area sown	77,424 hectare
Population	6,42,415 (2011)	Forests	1,304 sq. km
Population Density	244 per sq. km	Villages electrified	338
Villages	380 (375 inhabited)	Literacy rate	68%
Tehsil	7	Bank Branches	49
Towns	4	Principal Crop	Maize

Historical Places: Thanamandi, Dhandidhar Fort, Usman Memorial, Balidan Bhawan, War Memorial, Hall of Fame

Tourist Places: Nao Gazi Ziarat, Mangla Godess, Shahdara Sharif, Gum Sar, Chandan Sar, Samot Sar and Chingus.

SRINAGAR

At a Glance

Educational Institutions	955	Tehsil	2
Colleges/polytechnics	10	Towns	13
Universities	2	Blocks	1
Road length	1296 km	Live-Stock Population	2.50 lakh
Area	1183 sq. km	Gross Area sown	0.24 lakh hectare
Population	12,36,829 (2011)	Forests	660.50 sq. km
Population Density	613 per sq. km	Literacy rate	69.4%

Historical Places: Hazratbal Shrine, Shankaracharya Temple, Jama Masjid, Badshuhnun Dumat, Hari Parbat Fort, Khir Bhawani Temple,

Tourist Places: Srinagar district has many places of tourist attraction, visited by thousands of nature lovers and pleasure seekers. The Mughal gardens, laid out by kings who had a penchant for the beauty of Kashmir, are some of the few star attractions of the district. These are Shalimar Garden, Cheshma Shahi and Pari Mahal, Sonmarg, Dal Lake and Nishat Garden.

KISHTWAR

At a Glance

Area	7824 sq. km	Blocks	9
Population	2,30,696 (2011)	Literacy rate	56.2%
Population Density	140 per sq. km	Panchayats	134
Tehsil	4		

Historical Places: The area popularly known as *Land of Sapphire and Saffron.*

Tourist Places: Dul–Hasti Power projects.

REASI

At a Glance

Area	1700 sq. km	Blocks	4
Population	3,14,667 (2011)	Literacy rate	58.2%
Population Density	183 per sq. km	Panchayats	147
Tehsil	3		

Tourist Places: Bhimgarh Fort (Reasi Fort), Salal Hydro Electric Project.

BANDIPORA

At a Glance

Area	398 sq. km	Blocks	5
Population	3,92,232 (2011)	Literacy rate	56.3%
Population Density	1137 per sq. km	Panchayats	114
Tehsil	3	Villages	123

Historical Places: Bandipora is known as "Gate-way of Gilgit" and Astone. It is also called the 'Port of Wullar'.
Tourist Places: Wuller Lake.

KULGAM

At a Glance

Area	1067 sq. km	Blocks	6
Population	4,24,483 (2011)	Literacy rate	59.2%
Population Density	929 per sq. km	Panchayats	159
Tehsil	3	Villages	265

Tourist Places: Shrine of Hazrat Mir Syed Hussain, Ahrabal Water, Kulgam is considered as 'Rice-Bawl' of Kashmir.

RAMBAN

At a Glance

Area	1346 sq. km	Blocks	4
Population	2,83,713 (2011)	Literacy rate	54.3%
Population Density	213 per sq. km	Panchayats	124
Tehsil	2	Villages	116

Historical Places: Ramban town is situated on the right bank of River Chenab

SAMBA

At a Glance

Area	910 sq. km	Blocks	4
Population	3,18,898 (2011)	Literacy rate	81.4%
Population Density	319 per sq. km	Panchayats	100
Tehsil	1		

GANDERBAL

At a Glance

Area	1045 sq. km	Blocks	4
Population	2,97,446 (2011)	Literacy rate	58%
Population Density	1153 per sq. km	Panchayats	103
Tehsil	3		

Tourist Places: Sonamarg, Mansbal Lake, Qamar Sahib and Tulmulla Shrines

SHOPIAN

At a Glance

Area	312 sq. km	Blocks	2
Population	2,66,215 (2011)	Literacy rate	60.8%
Population Density	853 per sq. km	Panchayats	103
Tehsil	1		

LADAKH

Ladakh (UT) has 2 districts, Leh and Kargil.

LEH

At a Glance

Educational institutions	278	Panchayats	93
Health Institutions	167(Including ISM)	C.D. Blocks	9
Area	45,110 sq. km	Villages Covered Under	100 (3/95)
Population	1,33,487 (2011)	Area under HYV crop	17441 hectare
Population Density	3 per sq. km	Ration Card holders	16000
Villages	114	Villages electrified	75(3/95)
Tehsil	3	Literacy rate	77.2%
Town	1	Live Stock Population	397700

Historical Places: Hemis, Alchi, Spituk, Phyang, Shey, Thikse, Jama Masjid, Leh Palace.

KARGIL

At a Glance

Villages connected by Road	92	Panchayats	95
		Blocks	9
Area	14036 sq. km	Live-Stock Population	4 lakh
Population	1,40,802 (2011)	Forests	24 sq. km
Population Density	10 per sq. km	Literacy rate	71.3%
Villages	130	Bank Branches	11
Tehsil	3	Principal Crop	Barley Grim/
Towns	1		Wheat

Tourist Places: Suru Valley and Zanskar

❏ ❏ ❏

# Jammu & Kashmir Reorganisation

What is Article 370?

Article 370 of the Indian Constitution is *a 'temporary provision'* which grants special autonomous status to Jammu & Kashmir.

Under Part XXI of the Constitution of India, which deals with "Temporary, Transitional and Special provisions", the state of Jammu & Kashmir has been accorded special status under Article 370.

- All the provisions of the Constitution which are applicable to other states are not applicable to J&K.

Important provisions under the article

According to this article, except for defence, foreign affairs, finance and communications, Parliament needs the state government's concurrence for applying all other laws. Thus *the state's residents live under a separate set of laws, including those related to citizenship, ownership of property, and fundamental rights, as compared to other Indians.*

- *Indian citizens from other states cannot purchase land or property in Jammu & Kashmir.*

- Under Article 370, the *Centre has no power to declare financial emergency under Article 360 in the state.* It can declare emergency in the state only in case of war or external aggression. The Union government can therefore not declare emergency on grounds of internal disturbance or imminent danger unless it is made at the request or with the concurrence of the state government.

- Under Article 370, the *Indian Parliament cannot increase or reduce the borders of the state.*

- *The Jurisdiction of the Parliament of India in relation to Jammu and Kashmir is confined to the matters enumerated in the Union List, and also the concurrent list.* There is no State list for the State of Jammu and Kashmir.

- At the same time, while in relation to the other States, the residuary power of legislation belongs to Parliament, in the case of Jammu and Kashmir, the residuary powers belong to the Legislature of the State, except certain

- matters to which Parliament has exclusive powers such as preventing the activities relating to cession or secession, or disrupting the sovereignty or integrity of India.
- *The power to make laws related to preventive detention in Jammu and Kashmir belong to the Legislature of J & K and not the Indian Parliament.* Thus, no preventive detention law made in India extends to Jammu & Kashmir.
- *Part IV (Directive Principles of the State Policy) and Part IVA (Fundamental Duties) of the Constitution are not applicable to J&K.*

Jammu and Kashmir Reorganisation Act, 2019

- It is an act by the Indian Parliament where the State of Jammu and Kashmir was bifurcated into two union territories — Jammu & Kashmir and Ladakh.
    - The Union Territory of Jammu and Kashmir will have a legislative assembly,
    - Whereas the Union Territory of Ladakh will not have a legislative assembly and will be administered by the Lieutenant Governor alone.
- The Union Territory of Ladakh will include the districts Leh and Kargil which will, in effect, cease to be part of the existing state of Jammu and Kashmir.
- The remaining territories will remain with Jammu and Kashmir after the bifurcation.
- Representation in the House of People: Out of the six Lok Sabha seats in the state of Jammu and Kashmir, five will remain with the Union Territory of Jammu and Kashmir and one will go to the Union Territory of Ladakh.
- The Election Commission may conduct Lok Sabha elections for both the Union Territories as per the allocation of seats specified in the Delimitation of Parliamentary Constituencies Order, 1976 as amended by this act.

Legislative powers of the Union Territory of Jammu and Kashmir

- The Legislative Assembly may make laws for the whole or any part of the Union Territory of Jammu and Kashmir with respect to any of the matters enumerated in the state list except on subjects "public order" and "police" which will remain in the domain of the Centre vis-a-vis the LG.
- In case of inconsistencies between laws made by Parliament and laws made by the Legislative Assembly, earlier law shall prevail and law made by the Legislative Assembly shall be void.

Role and powers of the Lieutenant Governor

- The Governor of the existing State of Jammu and Kashmir shall be the Lieutenant Governor for the Union territory of Jammu and Kashmir, and the Union Territory of Ladakh for such period as may be determined by the President.

- Appointment of L-G in Ladakh: The President shall appoint the L-G under article 239.
- The L-G will be assisted by advisors appointed by the Centre since the Union Territory will not have a Legislative Assembly.
- In the case of Union Territory of Jammu and Kashmir, the L-G shall "act in his discretion" on issues which fall outside the purview of powers conferred on the Legislative Assembly, in which he is required to exercise any judicial functions, and/or matters related to All India services and the Anti-Corruption Bureau.

The Union Territory of Jammu and Kashmir

- The Jammu and Kashmir Legislative Assembly will have a tenure of five years unless it's dissolved earlier by the L-G.
- Provisions contained under Article 239a of the constitution that are applicable to Puducherry shall be applicable here as well.
  - This allows the Union Territory of Jammu and Kashmir to function as a legislative assembly under an administrator appointed under the said Article. In this case, it will be the LG.
- The delimitation of constituencies following the bifurcation may be determined by the Election Commission.
  - The constituencies will be reorganised through a de-limitation exercise under the 2002 Act of Parliament.
  - For the purpose of delimitation, the 2011 census figures will be taken as the benchmark.
- The number of seats in the Legislative Assembly of Jammu and Kashmir shall be increased from 107 to 114.
  - The state assembly currently has 111 seats, of which 46 are in the Valley, 37 in Jammu and the remaining four are in the Ladakh division.
  - Of these, 24 seats would be deemed to be vacant till the time Pakistan-Occupied Kashmir comes under the jurisdiction of the Indian state.
- With this, the existing legislative council in Jammu and Kashmir stands abolished. "Every member thereof ceases to be such member and all bills pending in the Legislative Council shall lapse."
- Four sitting members of the council of states (Rajya Sabha) representing the existing state of Jammu and Kashmir shall be deemed to have been elected to fill the seats allocated to the Union Territory of Jammu and Kashmir. Their term of office remaining unaltered.
- The High Court of the existing state of Jammu and Kashmir will be the common High Court of the two Union Territories.
- The new Assembly shall have reservations for Scheduled Caste and Tribes as in other parts of the state.

PART-I : PRELIMINARY

1. This Act may be called the Jammu and Kashmir Reorganisation Act, 2019.

2. In this Act, unless the context otherwise requires,—
   (*a*) "appointed day" means the day which the Central Government may, by notification in the Official Gazette, appoint;
   (*b*) "article" means an article of the Constitution;
   (*c*) "assembly constituency" and "parliamentary constituency" have the same meanings as in the Representation of the People Act, 1950 (43 of 1950);
   (*d*) "Election Commission" means the Election Commission appointed by the President under article 324;
   (*e*) "existing State of Jammu and Kashmir" means the State of Jammu and Kashmir as existing immediately before the appointed day, comprising the territory which immediately before the commencement of the Constitution of India in the Indian State of Jammu and Kashmir;
   (*f*) "law" includes any enactment, ordinance, regulation, order, bye-law, rule, scheme, notification or other instrument having, immediately before the appointed day, the force of law in the whole or in any part of the existing State of Jammu and Kashmir;
   (*g*) "Legislative Assembly" means Legislative Assembly of Union territory of Jammu and Kashmir;
   (*h*) "Lieutenant Governor" means the Adminstrator of the Union territory appointed by the President under artcle 239;
   (*i*) "notified order" means an order published in the Official Gazette;
   (*j*) "population ratio", in relation to the Union territory of Jammu and Kashmir, and Union territory of Ladakh means the ratio as per 2011 Census;
   (*k*) "Scheduled Castes" in relation to the Union territory means such castes, races or tribes or parts of groups within such castes, races or tribes as are deemed under article 341 to be Scheduled Castes in relation to that Union territory;
   (*l*) "Scheduled Tribes" in relation to the Union territory means such tribes or tribal communities or parts of or groups within such tribes or tribal communities as are deemed under article 342 to be Scheduled Tribes in relation to that Union territory;
   (*m*) "sitting member", in relation to either House of Parliament or of the Legislature of the existing State of Jammu and Kashmir, means a person who immediately before the appointed day, is a member of that House;
   (*n*) "Union territory", in relation to the existing State of Jammu and Kashmir, means the Union territory of Jammu and Kashmir or Union territory of Ladakh, as the case may be;
   (*o*) "transferred territory" means the territory which on the appointed day is transferred from the existing State of Jammu and Kashmir to Union territories formed under sections 3 and 4 of this Act; and
   (*p*) any reference to a district, tehsil or other territorial division of the existing State of Jammu and Kashmir shall be construed as a reference to the area comprised within that territorial division on the appointed day.

PART II: REORGANISATION OF THE STATE OF JAMMU AND KASHMIR

3. On and from the appointed day, there shall be formed a new Union territory to be known as the Union territory of Ladakh comprising the following territories of the existing State of Jammu and Kashmir, namely:—

   "Kargil and Leh districts",

   and thereupon the said territories shall cease to form part of the existing State of Jammu and Kashmir.

4. On and from the appointed day, there shall be formed a new Union territory to be known as the Union territory of Jammu and Kashmir comprising the territories of the existing State of Jammu and Kashmir other than those specified in section 3.

5. On and from the appointed day, the Governor of the existing State of Jammu and Kashmir shall be the Lieutenant Governor for the Union territory of Jammu and Kashmir, and Union territory of Ladakh for such period as may be determined by the President.

6. On and from the appointed day, in the First Schedule to the Constitution, under the heading— "I. THE STATES",—
   (*a*) entry 15 shall be deleted.
   (*b*) entries from 16 to 29 shall be renumbered as 15 to 28.
   (*c*) under the heading — "II. UNION TERRITORIES",— after entry 7, the following entries shall be inserted, namely:—

   "8. Jammu and Kashmir: The territories specified in section 4 of the Jammu and Kashmir Reorganization Act, 2019".

   "9. Ladakh: The territories specified in section 3 of the Jammu and Kashmir Reorganization Act, 2019".

7. Nothing in the foregoing provisions of this Part shall be deemed to affect the power of the Government of successor Union territory of Jammu and Kashmir to alter, after the appointed day, the name, area or boundaries of any district or other territorial division in that Union territory.

PART III: REPRESENTATION IN THE LEGISLATURES

The Council of States

8. On and from the appointed day, in the Fourth Schedule to the Constitution, in the Table,—
   (*a*) entry 21 shall be deleted;
   (*b*) entries 22 to 31 shall be renumbered as entries 21 to 30, respectively;
   (*c*) after entry 30, the following entry shall be inserted, namely:—
   "31. Jammu and Kashmir ....4"

9. (*a*) On and from the appointed day, four sitting members of the Council of States representing the existing State of Jammu and Kashmir shall be deemed to have been elected to fill the seats allotted to the Union territory of Jammu and Kashmir, as specified in the First Schedule to this Act.

   (*b*) The term of office of such sitting members shall remain unaltered.

The House of the People

10. On and from the appointed day, there shall be allocated five seats to the successor Union territory of Jammu and Kashmir and one seat to Union territory of Ladakh, in the House of the People, and the First Schedule to the Representation of the People Act, 1950 (43 of 1950) shall be deemed to be amended accordingly.

11. (*a*) On and from the appointed day, the Delimitation of Parliamentary Constituencies Order, 1976 shall stand amended as directed in the Second Schedule of this Act.

    (*b*) The Election Commission may conduct the elections to the House of the People for the Union territory of Jammu and Kashmir and Union territory of Ladakh as per the allocation of seats specified in the Delimitation of Parliamentary Constituencies Order, 1976 as amended by this Act.

12. (*a*) Every sitting member of the House of the People representing a constituency which, on the appointed day by virtue of the provisions of section 10, stands allotted, with or without alteration of boundaries, to the successor Union territory of Jammu and Kashmir or Union territory of Ladakh, as the case may be, shall be deemed to have been elected to the House of the People by that constituency as so allotted.

    (*b*) The term of office of such sitting members shall remain unaltered.

The Lieutenant Governor and The Legislative Assembly of Union Territory of Jammu and Kashmir

13. On and from the appointed day, the provisions contained in article 239A, which are applicable to "Union territory of Puducherry", shall also apply to the "Union territory of Jammu and Kashmir".

14. (1) There shall be an Administrator appointed under article 239 of the Constitution of India for the Union territory of Jammu and Kashmir and shall be designated as Lieutenant Governor of the said Union territory.

    (2) There shall be a Legislative Assembly for the Union territory of Jammu and Kashmir.

    (3) The total number of seats in the Legislative Assembly of the Union territory of Jammu and Kashmir to be filled by persons chosen by direct election shall be 107.

    (4) Nowithstanding anything contained in sub-section (3), until the area of the Union territory of Jammu and Kashmir under the occupation of

Pakistan ceases to be so occupied and the people residing in that area elect their representatives—

(a) twenty four seats in the Legislative Assembly of Union territory of Jammu and Kashmir shall remain vacant and shall not be taken into account for reckoning the total membership of the Assembly; and

(b) the said area and seats shall be excluded in delimiting the territorial constituencies as provided under PART V of this Act.

(5) On and from the appointed day, the Delimitation of Assembly Constituencies Order, 1995, as applicable to Union territory of Jammu and Kashmir, shall stand amended as directed in the Third Schedule of this act.

(6) Seats shall be reserved for the Scheduled Castes and the Scheduled Tribes in the Legislative Assembly of the Union territory of Jammu and Kashmir.

(7) The number of seats reserved for the Scheduled Castes and the Scheduled Tribes in the Legislative Assembly of the Union territory of Jammu and Kashmir under sub-section (6) shall bear, as nearly as may be, the same proportion to the total number of seats in the Assembly as the population of the Scheduled Castes in the Union territory of Jammu and Kashmir or of the Scheduled Tribes in the Union territory of Jammu and Kashmir, in respect of which seats are so reserved, bears to the total population of the Union territory of Jammu and Kashmir.

Explanation: In this sub-section, the expression "population" means the population as ascertained at the last preceding census of which the relevant figures have been published:

Provided that the reference in this Explanation to the last preceding census of which the relevant figures have been published shall, until the relevant figures for the first census taken after the year 2026 have been published, be construed as a reference to the 2011 census.

(8) Notwithstanding anything in sub-section (6), the reservation of seats for the Scheduled Castes or Scheduled Tribes in the Legislative Assembly of the Union territory of Jammu and Kashmir shall cease to have effect on the same date on which the reservation of seats for the Scheduled Castes or the Scheduled Tribes in the House of the People shall cease to have effect under article 334 of the Constitution of India:

(9) In the Second Schedule to the Representation of the People Act, 1950, under the heading :— "I. THE STATES:"

(a) "entry 10 shall be deleted".

(b) "entries 11 to 29 shall be renumbered as 10 to 28".

(10) In the Second Schedule to the Representation of the People Act, 1950 , under the heading :— "II. Union Territories"

(*a*) after entry 4, the following entries shall be inserted, namely:—

1	2	3	4	5	6	7
"5. Jammu and Kashmir	83	6	....	83	6	....."

(11) The provisions of articles 324 to 327 and 329 of the Constitution of India, shall apply in relation to the Union territory of Jammu and Kashmir, the Legislative Assembly and the members thereof as they apply, in relation to a State, the Legislative Assembly of a State and the members thereof respectively; and any reference in articles 326 and 329 to "appropriate Legislature" shall be deemed to be a reference to Parliament.

15. Notwithstanding anything in sub-section (3) of section 14 the Lieutenant Governor of the successor Union territory of Jammu and Kashmir may nominate two members to the Legislative Assembly to give representation to women, if in his opinion, women are not adequately represented in the Legislative Assembly.

16. A person shall not be qualified to be chosen to fill a seat in the Legislative Assembly unless he—
  (*a*) is a citizen of India and makes and subscribes before some person authorised in that behalf by the Election Commission an oath or affirmation according to the form set out for the purpose in the Fourth Schedule of this Act;
  (*b*) is not less than twenty-five years of age; and
  (*c*) Possesses such other qualifications as may be prescribed in that behalf by or under any law made by the Parliament.

17. The Legislative Assembly, unless sooner dissolved, shall continue for five years from the date appointed for its first meeting and no longer, and the expiration of the said period of five years shall operate as a dissolution of the Legislative Assembly: Provided that the said period may, while a Proclamation of Emergency issued under clause (1) of article 352 is in operation, be extended by the President by order for a period not exceeding one year at a time and not extending in any case beyond a period of six months after the Proclamation has ceased to operate.

18. (1) The Lieutenant Governor shall, from time to time, summon the Legislative Assembly to meet at such time and place as he thinks fit, but six months shall not intervene between its last sitting in one session and the date appointed for its first sitting in the next session.

  (2) The Lieutenant Governor may, from time to time,—
  (*a*) prorogue the House;
  (*b*) dissolve the Legislative Assembly.

19. (1) Legislative Assembly shall, as soon as may be, choose two members of the Assembly to be respectively Speaker and Deputy Speaker thereof and, so often as the office of Speaker or Deputy Speaker becomes vacant, the Assembly shall choose another member to be Speaker or Deputy Speaker, as the case may be.

(2) A member holding office as Speaker or Deputy Speaker of the Assembly—
   (*a*) shall vacate his office if he ceases to be a member of the Assembly;
   (*b*) may at any time by writing under his hand addressed, if such member is the Speaker, to the Deputy Speaker, and if such member is the Deputy Speaker, to the Speaker, resign his office;
   (*c*) may be removed from his office by a resolution of the Assembly passed by a majority of all the then members of the Assembly:

   Provided that no resolution for the purpose of clause (*c*) shall be moved unless at least fourteen days' notice has been given of the intention to move the resolution:

   Provided further that, whenever the Assembly is dissolved, the Speaker shall not vacate his office until immediately before the first meeting of the Assembly after the dissolution.

(3) While the office of Speaker is vacant, the duties of the office shall be performed by the Deputy Speaker or, if the office of Deputy Speaker is also vacant, by such member of the Legislative Assembly as may be determined by the rules of procedure of the Assembly.

(4) During the absence of the Speaker from any sitting of the Legislative Assembly, the Deputy Speaker, or, if he is also absent, such person as may be determined by the rules of procedure of the Assembly, or, if no such person is present, such other person as may be determined by the Legislative Assembly, shall act as Speaker.

(5) There shall be paid to the Speaker and the Deputy Speaker of the Legislative Assembly, such salaries and allowances as may respectively be fixed by the Legislative Assembly of the Union territory of Jammu and Kashmir by law and, until provision in that behalf is so made, such salaries and allowances as the Lieutenant Governor may, by order determine.

20. (1) At any sitting of the Legislative Assembly, while any resolution for the removal of the Speaker from his office is under consideration, the Speaker, or while any resolution for the removal of the Deputy Speaker, from his office is under consideration, the Deputy Speaker, shall not, though he is present, preside, and the provisions of sub-section (4) of section 19 shall apply in relation to every such sitting as they apply in relation to a sitting from which the Speaker or, as the case may be, the Deputy Speaker, is absent.

(2) The Speaker shall have the right to speak in, and otherwise to take part in the proceedings of, the Legislative Assembly while any resolution for his removal from office is under consideration in the Assembly and shall, notwithstanding anything in section 25, be entitled to vote only in the first instance on such resolution or on any other matter during such proceedings but not in the case of an equality of votes.

21. (1) At the commencement of the first session after each general election to the Legislative Assembly and at the commencement of the first session of each year, the Lieutenant Governor shall address the Legislative Assembly, and shall inform the Legislative Assembly of the causes of its summons.

    (2) Provision shall be made by the rules regulating the procedure of the Legislative Assembly for the allotment of time for the discussion of matters referred to in such address.

22. Every Minister and the Advocate-General for the Union territory of Jammu and Kashmir shall have the right to speak in, and otherwise to take part in the proceedings of, the Legislative Assembly, and to speak in, and otherwise to take part in the proceedings of, any committee of the Legislative Assembly of which he may be named a member, but shall not by virtue of this section be entitled to vote.

23. (1) The Lieutenant Governor may address the Legislative Assembly and may for that purpose require the attendance of members.

    (2) The Lieutenant Governor may also send messages to the Legislative Assembly whether with respect to a Bill then pending in the Legislative Assembly or otherwise, and when a message so sent, the Legislative Assembly shall with all convenient despatch consider any matter required by the message to be taken into consideration.

24. Every member of the Legislative Assembly shall, before taking his seat, make and subscribe before the Lieutenant Governor of the said Union territory, or some person appointed in that behalf by him, an oath or affirmation according to the form set out for the purpose in the Fourth Schedule of this Act.

25. (1) Save as otherwise provided in this Act, all questions at any sitting of the Legislative Assembly shall be determined by a majority of votes of the members present and voting, other than the Speaker or person acting as such.

    (2) The Speaker, or person acting as such, shall not vote in the first instance, but shall have and exercise a casting vote in the case of an equality of votes.

    (3) The Legislative Assembly shall have power to act notwithstanding any vacancy in the membership thereof, and any proceedings in the Legislative Assembly shall be valid notwithstanding that it is discovered subsequently that some person who was not entitled so to do, sat or voted or otherwise took part in the proceedings.

    (4) The quorum to constitute a meeting of the Legislative Assembly shall be ten members or one- tenth of the total number of members of the Legislative Assembly, which ever is greater.

    (5) If at any time during a meeting of the Legislative Assembly there is no quorum, it shall be the duty of the Speaker, or person acting as such, either to adjourn the Legislative Assembly or to suspend the meeting until there is a quorum.

26. (1) No person shall be a member both of Parliament and of the Legislative Assembly, and if a person is chosen a member both of Parliament and of such Assembly, then, at the expiration of such period as may be specified in the rules made by the President, that person's seat in Parliament shall become vacant, unless he has previously resigned his seat in the Legislative Assembly of the said Union territory.

(2) If a member of the Legislative Assembly—

(*a*) becomes subject to any of disqualification mentioned in section 27 or section 28 for membership of the Legislative Assembly; or

(*b*) resigns his seat by writing under his hand addressed to the Speaker, and his resignation is accepted by the Speaker, his seat shall thereupon become vacant.

(*3*) If for a period of sixty days a member of the Legislative Assembly is without permission of the Assembly absent from all meetings thereof, the Assembly may declare his seat vacant:

Provided that in computing the said period of sixty days, no account shall be taken of any period during which the Assembly is prorogued or is adjourned for more than four consecutive days.

27. (1) A person shall be disqualified for being chosen as, and for being, a member of the Legislative Assembly—

(*a*) if he holds any office of profit under the Government of India or the Government of any State or the Government of Union territory of Jammu and Kashmir or the Government or administration of any other Union territory or other than an office declared by law made by Parliament or by the Legislative Assembly not to disqualify its holder; or

(*b*) if he is for the time being disqualified for being chosen as, and for being, a member of either House of Parliament under the provisions of sub-clause (*b*), sub-clause

(*c*) or sub-clause (*d*) of clause (*1*) of article 102 or of any law made in pursuance of that article.

(2) For the purposes of this section, a person shall not be deemed to hold an office of profit under the Government of India or the Government of any State or the Government of Union Territory of Jammu and Kashmir or the Government of any other Union territory by reason only that he is a Minister either for the Union or for such State or Union territory.

(3) If any question arises as to whether a member of the Legislative Assembly becomes subject to any of disqualification under the provisions of sub-sections (*1*) and (*2*), the question shall be referred for the decision of the Lieutenant Governor and his decision shall be final.

(4) Before giving any decision on any such question, the Lieutenant Governor shall obtain the opinion of the Election Commission and shall act according to such opinion.

28. The provisions of the Tenth Schedule to the Constitution shall, subject to the necessary modifications (including modifications for construing references therein to the Legislative Assembly of a State, article 188, article 194 and article 212 as references, respectively, to the Legislative Assembly of Union territory of Jammu and Kashmir, as the case may be, section 24, section 30 and section 50 of this Act), apply to and in relation to the members of the Legislative Assembly of Union territory of Jammu and Kashmir as they apply to and in relation to the members of the Legislative Assembly of a State, and accordingly,—

    (*a*) the said Tenth Schedule as so modified shall be deemed to form part of this Act; and

    (*b*) a person shall be disqualified for being a member of the Legislative Assembly if he is so disqualified under the said Tenth Schedule as so modified.

29. If a person sits or votes as a member of the Legislative Assembly before he has complied with the requirements of section 24 or when he knows that he is not qualified or that he is disqualified for membership thereof, or that he is prohibited from doing so by the provisions of any law made by Parliament or the Legislative Assembly of the Union territory of Jammu and Kashmir, he shall be liable in respect of each day on which he so sits or votes to a penalty of five hundred rupees to be recovered as a debt due to the said Union territory.

30. (1) Subject to the provisions of this Act and to the rules and standing orders regulating the procedure of the Legislative Assembly, there shall be freedom of speech in the Legislative Assembly.

    (2) No member of the Legislative Assembly shall be liable to any proceedings in any court in respect of anything said or any vote given by him in the Assembly or any committee thereof, and no person shall be so liable in respect of the publication by or under the authority of such Assembly of any report, paper, votes or proceedings.

    (3) In other respects, the powers, privileges and immunities of the Legislative Assembly and of the members and the committees thereof shall be such as are for the time being enjoyed by the House of the People and its members and committees.

    (4) The provisions of sub-sections (*1*), (*2*) and (*3*) shall apply in relation to persons who by virtue of this Act have the right to speak in, and otherwise to take part in the proceedings of, the Legislative Assembly or any committee thereof as they apply in relation to members of the Legislative Assembly.

31. Members of the Legislative Assembly shall be entitled to receive such salaries and allowances as may from time to time be determined by the Legislative Assembly by law and, until provision in that behalf is so made, such salaries and allowances as the Lieutenant Governor may, by order determine.

32. (1) Subject to the provisions of this Act, the Legislative Assembly may make laws for the whole or any part of the Union territory of Jammu and Kashmir with respect to any of the matters enumerated in the State List except the subjects mentioned at entries 1 and 2, namely "Public Order" and "Police" respectively or the Concurrent List in the Seventh Schedule to the Constitution of India in so far as any such matter is applicable in relation to the Union territories.

(2) Nothing in sub-section (*1*) shall derogate from the powers conferred on Parliament by the Constitution to make laws with respect to any matter for the Union territory of Jammu and Kashmir or any part thereof.

33. The property of the Union shall, save in so far as Parliament may by law otherwise provide, be exempted from all taxes imposed by or under any law made by the Legislative Assembly or by or under any other law in force in the Union territory of Jammu and Kashmir:

Provided that nothing in this section shall, until Parliament by law otherwise provides, prevent any authority within the Union territory of Jammu and Kashmir from levying any tax on any property of the Union to which such property was immediately before the commencement of the Constitution liable or treated as liable, so long as that tax continues to be levied in that Union territory.

34. (1) The provisions of article 286, article 287 and article 288 shall apply in relation to any law passed by the Legislative Assembly with respect to any of the matters referred to in those articles as they apply in relation to any law passed by the Legislature of a State with respect to those matters.

(2) The provisions of article 304 shall, with the necessary modifications, apply in relation to any law passed by the Legislative Assembly with respect to any of the matters referred to in that article as they apply in relation to any law passed by the Legislature of a State with respect to those matters.

35. If any provision of a law made by the Legislative Assembly with respect to matters enumerated in the State List, in the Seventh Schedule to the Constitution is repugnant to any provision of a law made by Parliament with respect to that matter, whether passed before or after the law made by the Legislative Assembly, or, if any provision of a law made by the Legislative Assembly with respect to any matter enumerated in the Concurrent List in the Seventh Schedule to the Constitution is repugnant to any provision of any earlier law, other than a law made by the Legislative Assembly, with respect to that matter, then, in either case, the law made by Parliament, or, as the case may be, such earlier law shall prevail and the law made by the Legislative Assembly of the Union territory shall, to the extent of the repugnancy, be void:

Provided that if such law made by the Legislative Assembly has been reserved for the consideration of the President and has received his assent, such law shall prevail in the Union territory of Jammu & Kashmir:

Provided further that nothing in this section shall prevent Parliament from enacting at any time any law with respect to the same matter including a law adding to, amending, varying or repealing the law so made by the Legislative Assembly.

36. (1) A Bill or amendment shall not be introduced into, or moved in, the Legislative Assembly except on the recommendation of the Lieutenant Governor, if such Bill or Amendment makes provision for any of the following matters, namely:—

 (*a*) the imposition, abolition, remission, alteration or regulation of any tax;

 (*b*) the amendment of the law with respect to any financial obligations undertaken or to be undertaken by the Government of the Union territory;

 (*c*) the appropriation of moneys out of the Consolidated Fund of the Union territory;

 (*d*) the declaring of any expenditure to be expenditure charged on the Consolidated Fund of the Union territory or the increasing of the amount of any such expenditure;

 (*e*) the receipt of money on account of the Consolidated Fund of the Union territory or the public account of the Union territory or the custody or issue of such money or the audit of the account of the Union territory:

 Provided that no recommendation shall be required under this sub-section for the moving of an amendment making provision for the reduction or abolition of any tax.

 (2) A Bill or Amendment shall not be deemed to make provision for any of the matters aforesaid by reason only that it provides for the imposition of fines or other pecuniary penalties, or for the demand or payment of fees for licences or fees for services rendered, or by reason that it provides for the imposition, abolition, remission, alteration or regulation of any tax by any local authority or body for local purposes.

 (3) A Bill which, if enacted and brought into operation, would involve expenditure from the Consolidated Fund of Union territory shall not be passed by the Legislative Assembly of the Union territory unless the Lieutenant Governor has recommended to the Assembly, the consideration of the Bill.

37. (1) A Bill pending in the Legislative Assembly shall not lapse by reason of the prorogation of the Legislative Assembly.

 (2) A Bill which is pending in the Legislative Assembly shall lapse on dissolution of the Legislative Assembly.

38. When a Bill has been passed by the Legislative Assembly, it shall be presented to the Lieutenant Governor and the Lieutenant Governor shall declare either that he assents to the Bill or that he withholds assent therefrom or that he reserves the Bill for the consideration of the President:

Provided that the Lieutenant Governor may, as soon as possible after the presentation of the Bill to him for assent, return the Bill if it is not a Money Bill together with a message requesting that the Assembly will reconsider the

Bill or any specified provisions thereof, and, in particular, will consider the desirability of introducing any such amendments as he may recommend in his message and, when a Bill is so returned, the Assembly will reconsider the Bill accordingly, and if the Bill is passed again with or without amendment and presented to the Lieutenant Governor for assent, the Lieutenant Governor shall declare either that he assents to the Bill or that he reserves the Bill for the consideration of the President:

Provided further that the Lieutenant Governor shall not assent to, but shall reserve for the consideration of the President, any Bill which,—

(a) in the opinion of the Lieutenant Governor would, if it became law, so derogate from the powers of the High Court as to endanger the position which that Court is, by the Constitution, designed to fill; or

(b) relates to any of the matters specified in clause (1) of article 31A; or

(c) the President may, by order, direct to be reserved for his consideration.

Explanation.—For the purposes of this section and section 39, a Bill shall be deemed to be a Money Bill if it contains only provisions dealing with all or any of the matters specified in sub-section (1) of section 36 or any matter incidental to any of those matters and, in either case, there is endorsed thereon the certificate of the Speaker of the Legislative Assembly signed by him that it is a Money Bill.

39. When a Bill is reserved by Lieutenant Governor for the consideration of the President, the President shall declare either that he assents to the Bill or that he withholds assent therefrom:

Provided that where the Bill is not a Money Bill, the President may direct the Lieutenant Governor to return the Bill to the Legislative Assembly together with such a message as is mentioned in the first proviso to section 38 and, when a Bill is so returned, the Assembly shall reconsider it accordingly within a period of six months from the date of receipt of such message and, if it is again passed by the Assembly with or without amendment, it shall be presented again to the President for his consideration.

40. No Act of the Legislative Assembly and no provision in any such Act, shall be invalid by reason only that some previous sanction or recommendation required by this Act was not given, if assent to that Act was given by the Lieutenant Governor, or, on being reserved by the Lieutenant Governor for the consideration of the President, by the President.

41. (1) The Lieutenant Governor shall in respect of every financial year cause to be laid before the Legislative Assembly of the Union territory of Jammu and Kashmir, a statement of the estimated receipts and expenditure of the Union territory for that year, in this Part referred to as the "annual financial statement".

(2) The estimates of expenditure embodied in the annual financial statement shall show separately—

(*a*) the sums required to meet expenditure described by this Act as expenditure charged upon the Consolidated Fund of the Union territory of Jammu and Kashmir, and

(*b*) the sums required to meet other expenditure proposed to be made from the Consolidated Fund of the Union territory of Jammu and Kashmir; and shall distinguish expenditure on revenue account from other expenditure.

(3) The following expenditure shall be expenditure charged on the Consolidated Fund of the Union territory of Jammu and Kashmir:—

(*a*) the emoluments and allowances of the Lieutenant Governor and other expenditure relating to his office;

(*b*) the charges payable in respect of loans advanced to the Union territory of Jammu and Kashmir from the Consolidated Fund of India including interest, sinking fund charges and redemption charges, and other expenditure connected therewith;

(*c*) the salaries and allowances of the Speaker and the Deputy Speaker of the Legislative Assembly;

(*d*) expenditure in respect of the salaries and allowances of Judges of High Court of Jammu and Kashmir;

(*e*) any sums required to satisfy any judgment, decree or award of any court or arbitral tribunal;

(*f*) expenditure incurred by the Lieutenant Governor in the discharge of his special responsibility;

(*g*) any other expenditure declared by the Constitution or by law made by Parliament or by the Legislative Assembly of the Union territory of Jammu and Kashmir to be so charged.

42. (1) So much of the estimates as relates to expenditure charged upon the Consolidated Fund of Union territory of Jammu and Kashmir shall not be submitted to the vote of the Legislative Assembly, but nothing in this sub-section shall be construed as preventing the discussion in the Legislative Assembly of any of those estimates.

(2) So much of the said estimates as relates to other expenditure shall be submitted in the form of demands for grants to the Legislative Assembly, and the Legislative Assembly shall have power to assent, or to refuse to assent, to any demand, or to assent to any demand subject to a reduction of the amount specified therein.

(3) No demand for a grant shall be made except on the recommendation of the Lieutenant Governor.

43. (1) As soon as may be after the grants under section 42 have been made by the Legislative Assembly, there shall be introduced a Bill to provide for the appropriation out of the Consolidated Fund of the Union territory of all moneys required to meet—

(*a*) the grants so made by the Legislative Assembly, and

(*b*) the expenditure charged on the Consolidated Fund of the Union territory of Jammu and Kashmir but not exceeding in any case the amount shown in the statement previously laid before the Assembly.

(2) No amendment shall be proposed to any such Bill in the Legislative Assembly which will have the effect of varying the amount or altering the destination of any grant so made or of varying the amount of any expenditure charged on the Consolidated Fund of the Union territory of Jammu and Kashmir and the decision of the person presiding as to whether an amendment is inadmissible under this sub-section shall be final.

(3) Subject to the other provisions of this Act, no money shall be withdrawn from the Consolidated Fund of the Union territory except under appropriation made by law passed in accordance with the provisions of this section.

44. (1) The Lieutenant Governor shall—

(*a*) if the amount authorised by any law made in accordance with the provisions of section 43 to be expended for a particular service for the current financial year is found to be insufficient for the purposes of that year or when a need has arisen during the current financial year for supplementary or additional expenditure upon some new service not contemplated in the annual financial statement for that year, or

(*b*) if any money has been spent on any service during a financial year in excess of the amount granted for that service and for that year, cause to be laid before the Legislative Assembly, another statement showing the estimated amount of that expenditure or cause to be presented to the Legislative Assembly with such previous approval a demand for such excess, as the case may be.

(2) The provisions of sections 41, 42 and 43 shall have effect in relation to any such statement and expenditure or demand and also to any law to be made authorising the appropriation of moneys out of the Consolidated Fund of the Union territory of Jammu and Kashmir to meet such expenditure or the grant in respect of such demand as they have effect in relation to the annual financial statement and the expenditure mentioned therein or to a demand for a grant and the law to be made for the authorisation of appropriation of moneys out of the Consolidated Fund of the Union territory of Jammu and Kashmir to meet such expenditure or grant.

45. (1) Notwithstanding anything in the foregoing provisions of this Part, the Legislative Assembly shall have power to make any grant in advance in respect of the estimated expenditure for a part of any financial year pending the completion of the procedure prescribed in section 42 for the voting of such grant and the passing of the law in accordance with the provisions of section 43 in relation to that expenditure and the Legislative Assembly shall have power to authorise by law the withdrawal of moneys from the

Consolidated Fund of the Union territory of Jammu and Kashmir for the purposes for which the said grant is made.

(2) The provisions of sections 42 and 43 shall have effect in relation to the making of any grant under sub-section (*1*) or to any law to be made under that sub-section as they have effect in relation to the making of a grant with regard to any expenditure mentioned in the annual financial statement and the law to be made for the authorisation of appropriation of moneys out of the Consolidated Fund of the Union territory of Jammu and Kashmir to meet such expenditure.

46. (1) The Legislative Assembly may make rules for regulating, subject to the provisions of this Act, its procedure and the conduct of its business: Provided that the Lieutenant Governor shall, after consultation with the Speaker of the Legislative Assembly, make rules—

(*a*) for securing the timely completion of financial business;

(*b*) for regulating the procedure of, and the conduct of business in, the Legislative Assembly in relation to any financial matter or to any Bill for the appropriation of moneys out of the Consolidated Fund of the Union territory of Jammu and Kashmir;

(*c*) for prohibiting the discussion of, or the asking of questions on, any matter which affects the discharge of the functions of the Lieutenant Governor in so far as he is required by this Act to act in his discretion.

(2) Until rules are made under sub-section (*1*), the rules of procedure and standing orders in force immediately before the commencement of this Act, with respect to the Legislative Assembly of the existing State of Jammu and Kashmir shall have effect in relation to the Legislative Assembly of the Union territory of Jammu and Kashmir subject to such modifications and adaptations as may be made therein by the Speaker of Legislative Assembly.

47. (1) The Legislative Assembly may by law adopt any one or more of the languages in use in the Union territory of Jammu and Kashmir or Hindi as the official language or languages to be used for all or any of the official purposes of the Union territory of Jammu and Kashmir.

(2) The business in the Legislative Assembly of the Union territory of Jammu and Kashmir shall be transacted in the official language or languages of the Union territory of Jammu and Kashmir or in Hindi or in English:

Provided that the Speaker of the Legislative Assembly or person acting as such, as the case may be, may permit any member who cannot adequately express himself in any of the languages aforesaid to address the Legislative Assembly in his mothertongue.

48. Notwithstanding anything contained in section 47, until Parliament by law otherwise provides, the authoritative texts—

(*a*) of all Bills to be introduced or amendments thereto to be moved in the Legislative Assembly,

(*b*) of all Acts passed by the Legislative Assembly, and

(*c*) of all orders, rules, regulations and bye-laws issued under any law made by the Legislative Assembly of, shall be in the English language:

Provided that where the Legislative Assembly has prescribed any language other than the English language for use in Bills introduced in, or Acts passed by, the Legislative Assembly or in any order, rule, regulation or bye-law issued under any law made by the Legislative Assembly of the Union territory of Jammu and Kashmir, a translation of the same in the English language published under the authority of the Lieutenant Governor in the Official Gazette shall be deemed to be the authoritative text thereof in the English language.

49. No discussion shall take place in the Legislative Assembly with respect to the conduct of any judge of the Supreme Court or of a High Court in the discharge of his duties.

50. (1) The validity of any proceedings in the Legislative Assembly shall not be called in question on the ground of any alleged irregularity of procedure.

(2) No officer or member of the Legislative Assembly in whom powers are vested by or under this Act for regulating procedure or the conduct of business, or for maintaining order in the Legislative Assembly shall be subject to the jurisdiction of any court in respect of the exercise by him of those powers.

51. (1) Legislative Assembly shall have a separate secretariat staff.

(2) The Legislative Assembly may by law regulate the recruitment, and the conditions of service of persons appointed, to the secretarial staff of the Legislative Assembly.

(3) Until provision is made by the Legislative Assembly under sub-section (2), the Lieutenant Governor may, after consultation with the Speaker of the Legislative Assembly make rules regulating the recruitment, and the conditions of service of persons appointed, to the secretarial staff of the Assembly and any rules so made shall have effect subject to the provisions of any law made under the said sub-section.

52. (1) If at any time, except when the Legislative Assembly is in session, the Lieutenant Governor thereof is satisfied that circumstances exist which render it necessary for him to take immediate action, he may promulgate such Ordinances as the circumstances appear to him to require:

Provided that the power of making an Ordinance under this section shall extend only to those matters with respect to which the Legislative Assembly has power to make laws.

(2) An Ordinance promulgated under this section shall have the same force and effect as an Act of the Legislative Assembly assented by the Lieutenant Governor but every such Ordinance—

(*a*) Shall be laid before the Legislative Assembly and shall cease to operate at the expiration of six weeks from the re-assembly of the Legislative Assembly, or if before the expiration of that period a resolution disapproving it is passed by the Legislative Assembly; and

(*b*) May be withdrawn at any time by the Lieutenant Governor.

Council of Ministers for the Union territory of Jammu and Kashmir

53. (1) There shall be a Council of Ministers consisting of not more than ten percent of the total number of members in the Legislative Assembly, with the Chief Minister at the head to aid and advise the Lieutenant Governor in the exercise of his functions in relation to matters with respect to which the Legislative Assembly has power to make laws except in so far as he is required by or under this Act to act in his discretion or by or under any law to exercise any judicial or quasi-judicial functions.

(2) The Lieutenant Governor shall, in the exercise of his functions, act in his discretion in a matter:

(*i*) which falls outside the purview of the powers conferred on the Legislative Assembly; or

(*ii*) in which he is required by or under any law to act in his discretion or to exercise any judicial functions.

(*iii*) related to All India Services and Anti Corruption Bureau:

Provided that if any question arises whether any matter is or is not a matter as respects which the Lieutenant Governor is by or under this Act required to act in his discretion, the decision of the Lieutenant Governor in his discretion shall be final, and the validity of anything done by the Lieutenant Governor shall not be called in question on the ground that he ought or ought not to have acted in his discretion.

(3) The question whether any, and if so what, advice was tendered by Ministers to the Lieutenant Governor shall not be inquired into in any court.

54. (1) The Chief Minister shall be appointed by the Lieutenant Governor and the other Ministers shall be appointed by the Lieutenant Governor on the advice of the Chief Minister.

(2) The Ministers shall hold office during the pleasure of the Lieutenant Governor.

(3) The Council of Ministers shall be collectively responsible to the Legislative Assembly.

(4) Before a Minister enters upon his office, the Lieutenant Governor shall administer to him the oaths of office and of secrecy according to the forms set out for the purpose in the Fourth Schedule.

(5) A Minister who for any period of six consecutive months is not a member of the Legislative Assembly shall at the expiration of that period cease to be a Minister.

(6) The salaries and allowances of Ministers shall be such as the Legislative Assembly may from time to time by law determine, and until the Legislative Assembly so determines, shall be determined by the Lieutenant Governor.

55. (*1*) The Lieutenant Governor shall make rules on the advice of the Council of Ministers—

(*a*) for the allocation of business to the Ministers; and

(*b*) for the more convenient transaction of business with the Ministers including the procedure to be adopted in case of a difference of opinion between the Lieutenant Governor and the Council of Ministers or a Minister.

(2) Save as otherwise provided in this Act, all executive action of the Lieutenant Governor, whether taken on the advice of his Ministers or otherwise, shall be expressed to be taken in the name of the Lieutenant Governor.

(3) Orders and other instruments made and executed in the name of the Lieutenant Governor, shall be authenticated in such manner as may be specified in rules to be made by the Lieutenant Governor on the advice of council of ministers, and the validity of an order or instrument which is so authenticated shall not be called in question on the ground that it is not an order or instrument made or executed by the Lieutenant Governor.

56. It shall be the duty of the Chief Minister—

(*a*) to communicate to the Lieutenant Governor all decisions of the Council of Ministers relating to the administration of the affairs of the Union territory and proposals for legislation;

(*b*) to furnish such information relating to the administration of the affairs of the Union territory and proposals for legislation as Lieutenant Governor may call for.

Legislative Council

57. (1) Notwithstanding anything to the contrary contained in any law, document, judgment, ordinance, rule, regulation or notification, on and from the appointed day, the Legislative Council of the existing State of Jammu and Kashmir shall stand abolished.

(2) On the abolition of the Legislative Council, every member thereof shall ceased to be such member.

(3) All Bills pending in the Legislative Council immediately before the appointed day shall lapse on the abolition of the Council.

PART IV : ADMINISTRATION OF UNION TERRITORY OF LADAKH

58. (1) The Union territory of Ladakh will be administered by the President acting, to such extent as he thinks fit, through a Lieutenant Governor to be appointed by him under article 239.

(2) The President may make regulations for the peace, progress and good government of the Union territory of Ladakh under article 240 of the Constitution of India.

(3) Any regulation so made may repeal or amend any Act made by Parliament or any other law which is for the time being applicable to the Union territory of Ladakh and, when promulgated by the President, shall have the same force and effect as an Act of Parliament which applies to the Union territory of Ladakh.

(4) The Lieutenant Governor shall be assisted by advisor(s) to be appointed by the Central Government.

PART V : DELIMITATION OF CONSTITUENCIES

59. In this Part, unless the context otherwise requires,—

(*a*) "associate member" means a member associated with the Delimitation Commission under section 60;

(*b*) "Delimitation Commission" means the Delimitation Commission to be constituted under section 3 of the Delimitation Act, 2002; and thereafter by any law made by the Parliament.

(*c*) "Election Commission" means the Election Commission appointed by the President under article 324 of the Constitution of India;

(*d*) "latest census figures" mean the census figures ascertained at the latest census of which the finally published figures are available;

(*e*) "Parliamentary Constituency" means a constituency provided by law for the purpose of elections to the House of the People from Union territory of Jammu and Kashmir and Union territory of Ladakh.

(*f*) "Assembly Constituency" means a constituency provided by law for the purpose of elections to the Legislative Assembly.

60. (*1*) Without prejudice to sub-sections (*3*) of section 14 of this Act, the number of seats in the Legislative Assembly of Union territory of Jammu and Kashmir shall be increased from 107 to 114, and delimitation of the constituencies may be determined by the Election Commission in the manner hereinafter provided—

(*a*) the number of seats to be reserved for the Scheduled Castes and the Scheduled Tribes in the Legislative Assembly, having regard to the relevant provisions of the Constitution;

(*b*) the assembly constituencies into which the Union territory shall be divided, the extent of each of such constituencies and in which of them seats shall be reserved for the Scheduled Castes or for the Scheduled Tribes; and

(c) the adjustments in the boundaries and description of the extent of the parliamentary constituencies in each Union territory that may be necessary or expedient.

(2) In determining the matters referred to in clauses (b) and (c) of sub-section (1), the Election Commission shall have regard to the following provisions, namely:—

(a) all the constituencies shall be single-member constituencies;

(b) all constituencies shall, as far as practicable, be geographically compact areas, and in delimiting them, regard shall be had to physical features, existing boundaries of administrative units, facilities of communication and conveniences to the public; and

(c) constituencies in which seats are reserved for the Scheduled Castes and the Scheduled Tribes shall, as far as practicable, be located in areas where the proportion of their population to the total population is the largest.

(3) The Election Commission shall, for the purpose of assisting it in the performance of its functions under sub-section (1), associate with itself as associate members, four persons as the Central Government may by order specify, being persons who are the members of the Legislative Assembly of the Union territory of Jammu and Kashmir or four members of the House of the People representing the Union territory of Jammu and Kashmir:

Provided that none of the associate members shall have a right to vote or to sign any decision of the Election Commission.

(4) If, owing to death or resignation, the office of an associate member falls vacant, it shall be filled as far as practicable, in accordance with the provisions of sub-section (3).

(5) The Election Commission shall—

(a) publish its proposals for the delimitation of constituencies together with the dissenting proposals, if any, of any associate member who desires publication thereof in the Official Gazette and in such other manner as the Commission may consider fit, together with a notice inviting objections and suggestions in relation to the proposals and specifying a date on or after which the proposals will be further considered by it;

(b) consider all objections and suggestions which may have been received by it before the date so specified; and

(c) after considering all objections and suggestions which may have been received by it before the date so specified, determine by one or more orders the delimitation of constituencies and cause such order or orders to be published in the Official Gazette, and there upon such publication, the order or orders shall have the full force of law and shall not be called in question in any court.

(6) As soon as may be after such publication, every such order relating to assembly constituencies shall be laid before the Legislative Assembly of the Union territory of Jammu and Kashmir.

61. (1) The Election Commission may by notification in the Official Gazette,—

(*a*) correct any printing mistakes in any order made under section 60 or any error arising therein from inadvertent slip or omission; and

(*b*) where the boundaries or name of any territorial division mentioned in any such order or orders is or are altered, make such amendments as appear to it to be necessary or expedient for bringing such order up-to-date.

(2) Every notification under this section relating to an assembly constituency shall be laid, as soon as may be after it is issued, before the Legislative Assembly.

62. (1) On and from the appointed day, notwithstanding the publication of orders under sub-section (*1*) of section 10 of the Delimitation Act, 2002 or anything contained in sub-section (*2*) or sub-section (*4*) of the said section, the Delimitation Act, 2002 shall be deemed to have been amended as provided below:

(*a*) in section 2(*f*), the words "but does not include the State of Jammu and Kashmir" shall be omitted; and

(*b*) for the purpose of delimitation of Assembly and Parliamentary Constituencies, the words and figure "census held in the year 2001", wherever occurring, shall be construed as words and figure "census held in the year 2011".

(2) Readjustment of the constituencies as provided under section 60 in the successor Union territory of Jammu and Kashmir into Assembly Constituencies, shall be carried by the Delimitation Commission, to be constituted under the Delimitation Act, 2002 as amended by this Act, and shall take effect from such date as the Central Government may, by order, published in the Official Gazette, specify.

(3) Readjustment of the constituencies as provided under section 11 in the successor Union territory of Jammu and Kashmir into Parliamentary Constituencies, shall be carried by the Delimitation Commission, to be constituted under the Delimitation Act, 2002 as amended by this Act, and shall take effect from such date as the Central Government may, by order, published in the Official Gazette, specify.

63. Notwithstanding anything contained in sections 59 to 61, until the relevant figures for the first census taken after the year 2026 have been published, it shall not be necessary to readjust the division of successor Union territory of Jammu and Kashmir into Assembly and Parliamentary Constituencies and any reference to the "latest census figures" in this Part shall be construed as a reference to the 2011 census figures.

64. The procedure as provided in the law made by Parliament, shall apply, in relation to the delimitation of Parliamentary and Assembly constituencies under this Part as they apply in relation to the delimitation of Parliamentary and Assembly constituencies under that law.

PART VI : SCHEDULED CASTES AND SCHEDULED TRIBES

65. On and from the appointed day, the Constitution Jammu and Kashmir (Scheduled Castes) Order, 1956, shall stand applied to the Union territory of Jammu and Kashmir and Union territory of Ladakh.

66. On and from the appointed day, the Constitution Jammu and Kashmir (Scheduled Tribes) Order, 1989, shall stand applied to the Union territory of Jammu and Kashmir and Union territory of Ladakh.

PART VII : MISCELLANEOUS AND TRANSITIONAL PROVISIONS

67. (1) On and from the appointed day, all revenues received in the Union territory of Jammu and Kashmir by the Government of India or the Lieutenant Governor of the Union territory of Jammu and Kashmir in relation to any matter with respect to which the Legislative Assembly of the Union territory of Jammu and Kashmir has power to make laws, and all grants made and all loans advanced to the Union territory of Jammu and Kashmir from the Consolidated Fund of India and all loans raised by the Government of India or the Lieutenant Governor of the Union territory of Jammu and Kashmir upon the security of the Consolidated Fund of the Union territory of Jammu and Kashmir and all moneys received by the Union territory of Jammu and Kashmir in repayment of loans shall form one Consolidated Fund to be entitled "the Consolidated Fund of the Union territory of Jammu and Kashmir".

(2) No moneys out of such Consolidated Fund shall be appropriated except in accordance with, and for the purposes and in the manner provided in, this Act.

(3) The custody of such Consolidated Fund, the payment of moneys into such Funds, the withdrawal of moneys therefrom and all other matters connected with or ancillary to those matters shall be regulated by rules made by the Lieutenant Governor.

68. (1) On and from the appointed day, all other public moneys received by or on behalf of the Lieutenant Governor shall be credited to a Public Account entitled "the Public Account of the Union territory of Jammu and Kashmir".

(2) The custody of public moneys, other than those credited to the Consolidated Fund of the Union territory or the Contingency Fund of the

Union territory of Jammu and Kashmir, received by or on behalf of the Lieutenant Governor, their payment into the Public Accounts of the Union territory of Jammu and Kashmir and the withdrawal of moneys from such account and all other matters connected with or ancillary to the aforesaid matters shall be regulated by rules made by the Lieutenant Governor on the advice of Council of Ministers.

69. (1) There shall be established a Contingency Fund in the nature of an imprest to be entitled "the Contingency Fund of the Union territory of Jammu and Kashmir", into which shall be paid from and out of the Consolidated Fund of the Union territory of Jammu and Kashmir such sums as may, from time to time, be determined by law made by the Legislative Assembly of the Union territory of Jammu and Kashmir; and the said Fund shall be held by the Lieutenant Governor to enable advances to be made by him out of such Fund.

(2) No advances shall be made out of the Contingency Fund of the Union territory of Jammu and Kashmir except for the purposes of meeting unforeseen expenditure pending authorisation of such expenditure by the Legislative Assembly under appropriations made by law.

(3) The Lieutenant Governor on the advice of the Council of Ministers may make rules regulating all matters connected with or ancillary to the custody of, the payment of moneys into, and the withdrawal of moneys from, the Contingency Fund of the Union territory of Jammu and Kashmir.

70. (1) The executive power of the Union territory extends to borrowing upon the security of the Consolidated Fund of the Union territory of Jammu and Kashmir within such limits, if any, as may, from time to time, be fixed by Legislative assembly by law and to the giving of guarantees within such limits, if any, as may be so fixed.

(2) Any sums required for the purpose of invoking a guarantee shall be charged on the Consolidated Fund of the Union territory of Jammu and Kashmir.

71. The accounts of the Union territory of Jammu and Kashmir shall be kept in such form as the Lieutenant Governor may, after obtaining advice of the Comptroller and Auditor-General of India, prescribe by rules.

72. The reports of the Comptroller and Auditor-General of India relating to the accounts of Union territory of Jammu and Kashmir for any period subsequent to the date referred to in sub-section (*1*) of section 67 shall be submitted to the Lieutenant Governor who shall cause them to be laid before the Legislative Assembly.

73. If the President, on receipt of a report from the Lieutenant Governor of Union territory of Jammu and Kashmir, or otherwise, is satisfied,—

(*a*) that a situation has arisen in which the administration of the Union territory of Jammu and Kashmir cannot be carried on in accordance with the provisions of this Act, or (*b*) that for the proper administration of Union territory of Jammu and Kashmir it is necessary or expedient so to do, the President may, by order, suspend the operation of all or any of the provisions of this Act for such period as he thinks fit and make such incidental and consequential provisions as may appear to him to be necessary or expedient for administering the Union territory of Jammu and Kashmir in accordance with the provisions of this Act.

74. Where the Legislative Assembly is dissolved, or its functioning as such Assembly remains suspended, on account of an order under section 73, it shall be competent for the President to authorize, when the House of the People is not in session, expenditure from the Consolidated Fund of the Union territory of Jammu and Kashmir pending the sanction of such expenditure by Parliament.

PART VIII : HIGH COURT

75. (1) On and from the appointed day,—

(*a*) the High Court of Jammu and Kashmir shall be the common High Court for the Union territory of Jammu and Kashmir and Union territory of Ladakh;

(*b*) the Judges of the High Court of Jammu and Kashmir for the existing State of Jammu and Kashmir holding office immediately before the appointed day shall become on that day the Judges of the common High Court.

(2) The expenditure in respect of salaries and allowances of the Judges of the common High Court shall be allocated amongst the Union territory of Jammu and Kashmir and Union territory of Ladakh on the basis of population ratio.

76. (1) On and from the date referred to in sub-section (*1*) of section 75, in the Advocates Act, 1961, in section 3, in sub-section (*1*),—

(*a*) in clause (*a*), the words "Jammu and Kashmir" shall be deleted.

(*b*) after clause (*f*), the following clause shall be inserted, namely—

- (*g*) - for the Union territory of Jammu and Kashmir and Union territory of Ladakh, to be known as the Bar Council of Jammu and Kashmir; and Ladakh.

(2) Any person who immediately before the date referred to in sub-section (*1*) of section 75 is an advocate on the roll of the Bar Council of the existing State of Jammu and Kashmir and practising as an advocate in the High Court of Jammu and Kashmir, may continue to be members of the "Bar council of Jammu and Kashmir; and Ladakh", notwithstanding anything contained in the Advocates Act, 1961 and the rules made thereunder.

(3) The persons other than the advocates who are entitled immediately before the date referred to in sub-section (*1*) of section 75, on and after that date,

be recognised as such persons entitled also to practise in the common High Court of Jammu and Kashmir or any subordinate court thereof, as the case may be.

(4) The right of audience in the common High Court of Jammu and Kashmir shall be regulated in accordance with the like principles as immediately before the date referred to in sub-section (1) of section 75, are in force with respect to the right of audience in the High Court of Jammu and Kashmir.

77. Subject to the provisions of this Part, the law in force immediately before the date referred to in sub-section (1) of section 75 with respect to practice and procedure in the High Court of Jammu and Kashmir shall, with the necessary modifications, apply in relation to the common High Court of Jammu and Kashmir and accordingly, the common High Court of Jammu and Kashmir shall have all such powers to make rules and orders with respect to practice and procedure as are immediately before that date exercisable by the common High Court of Jammu and Kashmir:

Provided that any rules or orders which are in force immediately before the date referred to in sub-section (1) of section 75 with respect to practice and procedure in the High Court of Jammu and Kashmir shall, until varied or revoked by rules or orders made by the common High Court of Jammu and Kashmir, apply with the necessary modifications in relation to practice and procedure in the common High Court of Jammu and Kashmir as if made by that Court.

78. Nothing in this Part shall affect the application to the common High Court of Jammu and Kashmir of any provisions of the Constitution, and this Part shall have effect subject to any provision that may be made on or after the date referred to in sub-section (1) of section 75 with respect to the common High Court of Jammu and Kashmir by any Legislature or other authority having power to make such provision.

PART IX : ADVOCATE-GENERAL OF UNION TERRITORY OF JAMMU AND KASHMIR

79. (1) The Lieutenant Governor shall appoint a person who is qualified to be appointed a Judge of the High Court, to be Advocate-General for the Union territory of Jammu and Kashmir.

(2) It shall be the duty of such Advocate - General to give advice to the Government of such Union territory upon such legal matters and to perform such other duties of a legal character, as may from time to time be referred or assigned to him by the said Government, and to discharge the functions conferred on him by or under the Constitution or any other law for the time being in force.

(3) In the performance of his duties, the Advocate-General shall have the right of audience in all courts in the Union territory of Jammu and Kashmir.

(4) The Advocate-General shall hold office during the pleasure of the Lieutenant Governor and receive such remuneration as the Lieutenant Governor may determine.

PART X : AUTHORISATION OF EXPENDITURE AND DISTRIBUTION OF REVENUES

80. The Governor of existing State of Jammu and Kashmir may, at any time before the appointed day, authorise such expenditure from the Consolidated Fund of the Union territory of Jammu and Kashmir as he deems necessary for any period not more than six months beginning with the appointed day pending the sanction of such expenditure by the Legislative Assembly of the Union territory of Jammu and Kashmir:

Provided that the Lieutenant Governor of Union territory of Jammu and Kashmir may, after the appointed day, authorise such further expenditure as he deems necessary from the Consolidated Fund of the Union territory of Jammu and Kashmir for any period not extending beyond the said period of six months.

81. The Governor of existing State of Jammu and Kashmir may, at any time before the appointed day, authorise such expenditure from the Consolidated Fund of Union territory of Jammu and Kashmir as he deems necessary for any period not more than six months beginning with the appointed day pending the sanction of such expenditure by the Parliament:

Provided that the President may, after the appointed day, authorise such further expenditure as he deems necessary from the Consolidated Fund of India for any period not extending beyond the said period of six months.

82. (1) The reports of the Comptroller and Auditor-General of India referred to in clause (2) of article 151 relating to the accounts of the existing State of Jammu and Kashmir in respect of any period prior to the appointed day shall be submitted to the Lieutenant Governors of the successor Union territory of Jammu and Kashmir, and Union territory of Ladakh.

(2) The Lieutenant Governor of Jammu and Kashmir, thereafter shall cause the reports to be laid before the Legislature of the Union territory of Jammu and Kashmir.

(3) The Lieutenant Governor of Jammu and Kashmir may by order—

    (*a*) declare any expenditure incurred out of the Consolidated Fund of Jammu and Kashmir on any service in respect of any period prior to the appointed day during the financial year or in respect of any earlier financial year in excess of the amount granted for that service and for that year as disclosed in the reports referred to in sub-section (*1*) to have been duly authorised; and

    (*b*) provide for any action to be taken on any matter arising out of the said reports.

83. (1) The award made by the Fourteenth Finance Commission to the existing State of Jammu and Kashmir shall be apportioned between the successor Union territory of Jammu and Kashmir; and Union territory of Ladakh by the Central Government on the basis of population ratio and other parameters:

Provided that on the appointed day, the President shall make a reference to the Union Territories Finance Commission to take into account the resources available to the successor Union territory of Ladakh and make separate award for the successor Union territory of Ladakh:

Provided that on the appointed day, the President shall make a reference to the Fifteenth Finance Commission to include Union territory of Jammu and Kashmir in its Terms of Reference and make award for the successor Union territory of Jammu and Kashmir.

(2) Notwithstanding anything in sub-section (*1*), the Central Government may, having regard to the resources available to the successor Union territory of Ladakh make appropriate grants and also ensure that adequate benefits and incentives in the form of special development package are given to the backward areas of this region.

PART XI : APPORTIONMENT OF ASSETS AND LIABILITIES

84. (1) The provisions of this Part shall apply in relation to the apportionment of the assets and liabilities of the existing State of Jammu and Kashmir immediately before the appointed day, between the successor Union territory of Jammu and Kashmir and successor Union territory of Ladakh.

(2) The apportionment of the assets and liabilities of the existing State of Jammu and Kashmir shall be subject to the recommendations of a committee constituted by the Central Government.

(3) The process of apportionment shall be completed within a period of twelve months from the appointed day.

PART XII : PROVISIONS AS TO CERTAIN CORPORATIONS AND ANY OTHER MATTERS

85. (1) The Central Government may by order, establish one or more Advisory Committees within a period of 90 days from the appointed day, for the purposes of :

(*a*) apportionment of assets, rights and liabilities of the companies and corporations constituted for the existing State of Jammu and Kashmir between Union territory of Jammu and Kashmir and Union territory of Ladakh;

(*b*) issues relating to Continuance of arrangements in regard to generation and supply of electric power and supply of water;

(*c*) issues related to Jammu and Kashmir State Financial Corporation;

(*d*) issues related to Companies constituted for the existing state of Jammu and Kashmir regarding the division of the interests and shares and reconstitution of Board of Directors;

(*e*) issues related to facilities in certain State Institutions; and

(*f*) issues related to any other matters not covered under this section.

(2) The committees so appointed under sub-section (*1*) of this section, shall submit their reports within six months to the Lieutenant Governor of Union territory of Jammu and Kashmir, who shall act on the recommendations of such committees within a period of 30 days from the date of receiving such reports.

86. (1) Notwithstanding anything contained in section 88 of the Motor Vehicles Act, 1988, a permit granted by the State Transport Authority of the existing State of Jammu and Kashmir or any Regional Transport Authority in that State shall, if such permit was, immediately before the appointed day, valid and effective in any area in the transferred territory, be deemed to continue to be valid and effective in that area after that day till its period of validity subject to the provisions of that Act as for the time being in force in that area; and it shall not be necessary for any such permit to be countersigned by the Transport Authority of any of Union territory or any Regional Transport Authority therein for the purpose of validating it for use in such area:

Provided that the Lieutenant Governor may add to amend or vary the conditions attached to the permit by the Authority by which the permit was granted.

(2) No tolls, entrance fees or other charges of a like nature shall be levied after the appointed day in respect of any transport vehicle for its operations in any of the successor Union Territories under any such permit, if such vehicle was, immediately before that day, exempt from the payment of any such toll, entrance fees or other charges for its operations in the transferred territory:

Provided that the Central Government may, after consultation with the Government of Union territory of Jammu and Kashmir or the administration of Union territory of Ladakh, as the case may be, authorise the levy of any such toll, entrance fees or other charges, as the case may be:

Provided further that the provisions of this sub-section shall not be applicable where any such tolls, entrance fees or other charges of a like nature are leviable for the use of any road or bridge which is constructed or developed for commercial purpose by the State Government, an undertaking of the State Government, a joint undertaking in which the State Government is a shareholder or the private sector.

87. Where the assets, rights and liabilities of any body corporate carrying on business are, under the provisions of this Part, transferred to any other bodies corporate which after the transfer carry on the same business, the losses or profits or gains sustained by the body corporate first-mentioned which, but for such transfer, would have been allowed to be carried forward and set off in accordance with the provisions of Chapter VI of the Income-tax Act, 1961, shall be apportioned amongst the transferee bodies corporate in accordance with the rules to be made by the Central Government in this behalf and, upon such apportionment, the share of loss allotted to each transferee body corporate shall be dealt with in accordance with the provisions of Chapter VI of the said Act, as if the transferee body corporate had itself sustained such loss in a business carried on by it in the years in which those losses were sustained.

PART XIII : PROVISIONS AS TO SERVICES

88. (1) In this section, the expression "State cadre"—

   (*a*) in relation to the Indian Administrative Service, has the same meaning assigned to it in the Indian Administrative Service (Cadre) Rules, 1954;

   (*b*) in relation to the Indian Police Service, has the same meaning assigned to it in the Indian Police Service (Cadre) Rules, 1954; and

   (*c*) in relation to the Indian Forest Service, has the same meaning assigned to it in the Indian Forest Service (Cadre) Rules, 1966.

   (2) The members of the cadres of Indian Administrative Service, Indian Police Service and Indian Forest Service for the existing State of Jammu and Kashmir, on and from the appointed day, shall continue to function on the existing cadres.

   (3) The provisional strength, composition and allocation of officers currently borne on the existing cadre of Jammu and Kashmir to the Union territory of Jammu and Kashmir and Union territory of Ladakh, as referred to in sub-section (2) shall be such as the Lieutenant Governor of Union territory of Jammu and Kashmir may, by order, determine on or after the appointed day.

   (4) The members of each of the said services, currently borne on the Jammu and Kashmir cadre immediately before the appointed day shall be finally allocated between the successor Union territory of Jammu and Kashmir and Union territory of Ladakh, in such manner and with effect from such date or dates as the Central Government may, by order, specify on the recommendation of Lieutenant Governors of Union territory of Jammu and Kashmir; and Union territory of Ladakh.

   (5) The Officers so allocated to both the Union Territories shall function within these Union Teritories, in accordance with the rules framed by the Central Government.

(*6*) In future, the All India Service officers to be posted to Union territory of Jammu and Kashmir or Union territory of Ladakh, as the case may be, shall be borne on the Arunachal Goa Mizoram Union Territory cadre, and necessary modifications in corresponding cadre allocations rules may be made accordingly, by the Central Government.

89. (1) Every person who immediately before the appointed day is serving on substantive basis in connection with the affairs of the existing State of Jammu and Kashmir shall, on and from that day provisionally continue to serve in connection with the affairs of the Union territory of Jammu and Kashmir and Union territory of Ladakh, by general or special order of the Lieutenant Governor of Union territory of Jammu and Kashmir:

Provided that every direction under this sub-section issued after the expiry of a period of one year from the appointed day shall be issued with the consultation of the Government or Administartion of the successor Union Territories, as the case may be.

(2) As soon as may be after the appointed day, the Lieutenant Governor of Jammu and Kashmir shall, by general or special order, determine the successor Union territory to which every person referred to in sub-section (*1*) shall be finally allotted for service, after consideration of option received by seeking option from the employees, and the date with effect from which such allotment shall take effect or be deemed to have taken effect:

Provided that even after the allocation has been made, Lieutenant Governor of Union territory of Jammu and Kashmir may in order to meet any deficiency in the service, depute officers from one successor Union territory to the other Union territory.

(3) Every person who is finally allotted under the provisions of sub-section (2) to a successor Union territory shall, if he is not already serving therein, be made available for serving in the successor Union territory from such date as may be agreed upon between the Government of the successor Union territory of Jammu and Kashmir and Administration of Union territory of Ladakh, or, in default of such agreement, as may be determined by the Central Government:

Provided that the Central Government shall have the power to review any of its orders issued under this section.

90. (1) Nothing in this section or in section 89 shall be deemed to affect, on or after the appointed day, the operation of the provisions of Chapter I of Part XIV of the Constitution in relation to determination of the conditions of service of persons serving in connection with the affairs of the Union or any Union territory:

Provided that the conditions of service applicable immediately before the appointed day in the case of any person deemed to have been allocated to the Union territory of Jammu and Kashmir or Union territory of Ladakh under section 89 shall not be varied to his disadvantage except with the previous approval of the Lieutenant Governor.

(2) All services prior to the appointed day rendered by a person,—

    (*a*) if he is deemed to have been allocated to any Union territory under section 89, shall be deemed to have been rendered in connection with the affairs of that Union territory;

    (*b*) if he is deemed to have been allocated to the Union in connection with the administration of the successor Union territory, shall be deemed to have been rendered in connection with the affairs of the Union, for the purposes of the rules regulating his conditions of service.

(3) The provisions of section 89 shall not apply in relation to members of any All-India Service.

91. Every person who, immediately before the appointed day, is holding or discharging the duties of any post or office in connection with the affairs of the existing State of Jammu and Kashmir in any area which on that day falls within one of the successor Union territory shall continue to hold the same post or office in that successor Union territory, and shall be deemed, on and from that day, to have been duly appointed to the post or office by the Government of, or other appropriate authority in, that successor Union territory: Provided that nothing in this section shall be deemed to prevent a competent authority, on and from the appointed day, from passing in relation to such person any order affecting the continuance in such post or office.

92. On and from the appointed day, the employees of State Public Sector Undertakings, corporations and other autonomous bodies shall continue to function in such undertaking, corporation or autonomous bodies for a period of one year and during this period the corporate body concerned shall determine the modalities for distributing the personnel between the successor Union Territories.

93. (1) The Public Service Commission for the existing State of Jammu and Kashmir shall, on and from the appointed day, be the Public Service Commission for the Union territory of Jammu and Kashmir.

    (2) The Union Public Service Commission, with the approval of the President, shall serve the needs of the Union territory of Ladakh.

    (3) The persons holding office immediately before the appointed day as the Chairman or other member of the Public Service Commission for the existing State of Jammu and Kashmir shall, as from the appointed day, be the Chairman or, as the case may be, the other member of the Public Service Commission for the Union territory of Jammu and Kashmir.

    (4) Every person who becomes the Chairman or other member of the Public Service Commission for the Union territory of Jammu and Kashmir on the appointed day under subsection (*3*) shall be entitled to receive from the Government of the Union territory of Jammu and Kashmir, conditions of service not less favourable than those to which he was entitled under the provisions applicable to him.

(*5*) The report of the Jammu and Kashmir Public Service Commission as to the work done by the Commission in respect of any period prior to the appointed day shall be presented to the Lieutenant Governor of the State of Jammu and Kashmir, and the Lieutenant Governor of the Union territory of Jammu and Kashmir shall, on receipt of such report, cause a copy thereof together with a memorandum explaining as far as possible, as respects the cases, if any, where the advice of the Commission was not accepted, the reasons for such nonacceptance to be laid before the Legislature of the Union territory of Jammu and Kashmir.

PART XIV : LEGAL AND MISCELLANEOUS PROVISIONS

94. On and from the appointed day, in section 15 of the States Reorganisation Act, 1956, in clause (*a*), for the words "Jammu and Kashmir" the words "Union territory of Jammu and Kashmir and Union territory of Ladakh" shall be substituted.

95. (1) All Central laws in Table -1 of the Fifth Schedule to this Act, on and from the appointed day, shall apply in the manner as provided therein, to the Union territory of Jammu and Kashmir and Union territory of Ladakh.

(2) All other laws in Fifth Schedule, applicable to existing State of Jammu and Kashmir immediately before the appointed day, shall apply in the manner as provided therein, to the Union territory of Jammu and Kashmir and Union territory of Ladakh.

96. For the purpose of facilitating the application in relation to the successor Union Territories, of any law made before the appointed day, as detailed in Fifth Schedule, the Central Government may, before the expiration of one year from that day, by order, make such adaptations and modifications of the law, whether by way of repeal or amendment, as may be necessary or expedient, and thereupon every such law shall have effect subject to the adaptations and modifications so made until altered, repealed or amended by a competent Legislature or other competent authority.

97. Notwithstanding that no provision or insufficient provision has been made under section 96 for the adaptation of a law made before the appointed day, any court, tribunal or authority, required or empowered to enforce such law may, for the purpose of facilitating its application in relation to the Union territory of Jammu and Kashmir or Union territory of Ladakh, construe the law in such manner, without affecting the substance, as may be necessary or proper in regard to the matter before the court, tribunal or authority.

98. The Lieutenant Governor, as respects the concerned territory may, by notification in the Official Gazette, specify the authority, officer or person who, on or after the appointed day, shall be competent to exercise such functions exercisable under any law in force on that day as may be mentioned in that notification and such law shall have effect accordingly.

99. Where, immediately before the appointed day, the existing State of Jammu and Kashmir is a party to any legal proceedings with respect to any property, rights or liabilities subject to apportionment among the successor Union Territories under this Act, the Union territory of Jammu and Kashmir or the

Union territory of Ladakh which succeeds to, or acquires a share in, that property or those rights or liabilities by virtue of any provision of this Act shall be deemed to be substituted for the existing State of Jammu and Kashmir or added as a party to those proceedings, and the proceedings may continue accordingly.

100. (1) Every proceeding pending immediately before the appointed day before a court (other than High Court), tribunal, authority or officer in any area which on that day falls within the State of Jammu and Kashmir shall, if it is a proceeding relating exclusively to the territory, which as from that day are the territories of any Union territory, stand transferred to the corresponding court, tribunal, authority or officer of that Union territory.

(2) If any question arises as to whether any proceeding should stand transferred under sub-section (*1*), it shall be referred to the common High Court of Jammu and Kashmir and the decision of that High Court shall be final.

(3) In this section—

(*a*) proceeding includes any suit, case or appeal; and

(*b*) corresponding court, tribunal authority or officer in any of Union territory means—

(*i*) the court, tribunal, authority or officer in which, or before whom, the proceeding would have laid if it had been instituted after the appointed day; or

(*ii*) in case of doubt, such court, tribunal, authority, or officer in that Union territory, as may be determined after the appointed day by the Government or administration of that Union territory, or the Central Government, as the case may be, or before the appointed day by the Government of the existing State of Jammu and Kashmir to be the corresponding court, tribunal, authority or officer.

101. Any person who, immediately before the appointed day, is enrolled as a pleader entitled to practise in any subordinate court in the existing State of Jammu and Kashmir shall, for a period of one year from that day, continue to be entitled to practise in those courts, notwithstanding that the whole or any part of the territories within the jurisdiction of those courts has been transferred to any of the Union Territories.

102. The provisions of this Act shall have effect notwithstanding anything inconsistent therewith contained in any other law.

103. (1) If any difficulty arises in giving effect to the provisions of this Act, the President may, by order do anything not inconsistent with such provisions which appears to him to be necessary or expedient for the purpose of removing the difficulty:

Provided that no such order shall be made after the expiry of a period of five years from the appointed day.

(2) Every order made under this section shall be laid before each House of Parliament.

❏ ❏ ❏

Heads of the State/ Heads of the Government

HEADS OF THE STATE (SINCE AUGUST-1947)

NAME OF THE PERSON		TENURE
1.	Maharaja Hari Singh	–	Up to 20-06-1949
2.	Dr. Karan Singh	–	20-06-1949 to 17-11-1952
3.	Dr. Karan Singh	–	17-11-1952 to 09-04-1965
4.	Dr. Karan Singh (Governor)	–	10-04-1965 to 15-03-1967
5.	Chief Justice of J&K High Court was the acting Governor	–	15-03-1967 to 15-05-1967
6.	Sh. Bhagwan Sahay (Governor)	–	15-05-1967 to 03-07-1973
7.	Sh. L.K. Jha (Governor)	–	03-07-1973 to 26-02-1981
8.	Sh. B.K. Nehru (Governor)	–	26-02-1981 to 26-09-1984
9.	Sh. Jag Mohan (Governor)	–	26-09-1984 to 11-07-1989
10.	Gen. K.V. Krishna Rao (Governor)	–	11-07-1989 to 19-01-1990
11.	Sh. Jag Mohan (Governor)	–	19-01-1990 to 26-05-1990
12.	Sh. G.C. Saxena (Governor)	–	26-05-1990 to 12-03-1993
13.	Gen. K.V. Krishna Rao (Governor)	–	12-03-1993 to 02-05-1998
14.	Sh. G.C. Saxena (Governor)	–	02-05-1998 to 02-05-2003
15.	Lt. Gen. S.K. Sinha (Governor)	–	02-05-2003 to 25-06-2008
16.	Sh. N.N. Vohra (Governor)	–	25-06-2008 to 23-08-2018
17.	Sh. Satya Pal Malik (Governor)	–	23-08-2018 to 30-10-2019

HEADS OF THE GOVERNMENT (SINCE AUGUST-1947)

1.	Justice Mehar Chand Mahajan (PM)	–	15-10-1947 to 30-10-1947
2.	Sheikh Mohd Abdullah (Head of Emergency Govt.)	–	30-10-1947 to 05-03-1948
3.	Sheikh Mohammad Abdullah (PM)	–	05-03-1948 to August, 1953
4.	Bakshi Gh. Mohammad (PM)	–	August, 1953 to Oct., 1963

NAME OF THE PERSON		TENURE
5.	Kh. Shamsud-din (PM)	– Oct. 1963 to Feb. 1964
6.	Mr. Gh. Mohd. Sadiq (PM)	– Feb. 1964 to April, 1965
7.	Mr. Gh. Mohd. Sadiq (CM)	– April 1965 to Dec. 1971
8.	Syed Mir Qasim (CM)	– Dec. 1971 to Feb. 1975
9.	Shiekh Mohd. Abdullah (CM)	– Feb. 1975 to Sept. 1982
10.	Dr. Farooq Abdullah (CM)	– Sept. 1982 to July, 1984
11.	Mr. Gh. Mohd. Shah (CM)	– July, 1984 to March, 1986
12.	Dr. Farooq Abdullah (CM)	– Nov. 1986 to 19-01-1990
13.	Dr. Farooq Abdullah (CM)	– 09-10-1996 to Nov. 2002
14.	Mr. Mufti Mohd. Sayeed (CM)	– 02-11-2002 to Nov. 2005
15.	Mr. Gh. Nabi Azad (CM)	– Nov. 2005 to 07-07-2008.
16.	Mr. Omar Abdullah (CM)	– 05-01-2009 to 08-01-2015
17.	Mr. Mufti Mohd. Sayeed (CM)	– 01-03-2015 to 07-01-2016
18.	Ms. Mehbooba Mufti (CM)	– 04-04-2016 to 19-06-2018

**For Latest Information Refer to Who's Who &
Current Affairs Section in the beginning of the Book**

❑ ❑ ❑

17 Judiciary

J & K HIGH COURT

HISTORY

The full-fledged High Court of Judicature for the Jammu and Kashmir State was established in the year 1928. Prior to the establishment of High Court of Judicature. The Ruler of the State (Maharaja) was the final authority in the administration of justice. In the year 1889, the British Government asked the then Ruler of the State, Maharaja Partap Singh to appoint a Council and the Judicial member of the Council exercised all the appellate powers both on civil and criminal side. The State having two provinces - Jammu and Kashmir, had chief judges exercising judicial authority but they acted under the superintendence and control of the Law member of the Council. Later the Council was abolished and a Minister designated as Judge of the High Court was appointed by the Ruler to decide judicial cases. In 1927 a new Constitution was sanctioned by the then Ruler of the State and instead of Law Member, a Ministry in the Judicial Department was created.

Thereafter, in 1928, by virtue of Order No. 1 dated 26.3.1928, the High Court of Judicature was established and for the first time the High Court was to consist of The Chief Justice and two Judges. On 26.3.1928, the Maharaja appointed Lala Kanwar Sein as the First Chief Justice of the Court and Rai Bahadur Lala Bodh Raj Sawhney and Khan Sahib Aga Syed Hussain as Puisne Judges- The usual places of sitting of the High Court uses to be Jammu and Sri nagar.

In 1939 the Ruler promulgated the Constitution Act of 1996 which incorporated the provisions of law relating to the High Court and conferred upon the High Court a substantial measure of Independence. The High Court was invested with powers of superintendence and control over the Courts / District judiciary.

The 1996 (1939 A.D.) Act also constituted a 3 members Board of Judicial Advisers akin to the Privy Council in British India. The Board was to advise the Ruler in the disposal of the civil and criminal appeals against the decisions of the High Court. The Board of Judicial Advisers at the time of its abolition by the Constitution Act 1956 had 17 appeals pending before it. On request of the Chief Justice, the Government of India in consultation with the Chief Justice of India, constituted a Special Bench of the Supreme Court of India consisting of Justice Mehar Chand Mahajan, chief Justice of India, Justice S.R.D as and Justice Ghulam

Hassan for disposing off the pending 17 appeals. The Bench heard the appeals in Sri nagar and upheld the judgment of the High court in all the 17 appeals. It was a historical event, when a Bench of Supreme Court held sitting outside the place of seat at Delhi till date this is the sole instance. On 10.9.1943, Letters Patent was conferred on the High Court.

In 1954 vide Constitution Application Order of 1954, the jurisdiction of the Supreme Court was extended to the State of J&K. Under Art.32(2-A) of the Constitution of India, the State High Court was for the first time given power to issue writs for enforcement of the fundamental rights so far as they are applicable to the State of J&K. In 1957, by the Jammu and Kashmir Constitution Act, an independent judicial body with the High Court of Judicature at the top was created.

The High Court has at present a sanctioned strength of 17 Judges including 13 Permanent Judges and 4 Additional Judges. From May to end October, the Chief Justice and the Administrative Wing of High Court shifts to Srinagar and from November to end April, the HQ is at Jammu. However, Court sections of both the Jammu and Srinagar Wings of the High Court function throughout of the year.

In August 2019, a Reorganisation Bill was passed by both house of the Indian Parliament. The provision contained in the bill reorganised the state of Jammu & Kashmir into too union territories; Jammu & Kashmir (Union territory) and Ladakh (Union territory) with effect from 31 October 2019. The existing Jammu and Kashmir High curt is to continue as the high court for both union territories.

FORMER CHIEF JUSTICES

1. **Hon'ble Justice Kanwar Sain:** 27-04-1928 to 16-02-1931
2. **Hon'ble Justice Sir Birjor Dalal:** 16-02-1931 to 24-11-1936
3. **Hon'ble Justice Abdul Qayoom:** 24-11-1936 to 20-07-1940
4. **Hon'ble Justice Rachpal Singh:** 13-08-1940 to 06-03-1942
5. **Hon'ble Justice Ganga Nath:** 24-06-I942 to 23-10-1945
6. **Hon'ble Justice Sir S.K. Ghose:** 29-03-1946 to 29-03-1948
7. **Hon'bleJustice Janki Nath Wazir:** 30-03-1948 to 02-12-1967
8. **Hon'ble Justice Syed Murtaza Fazl Ali:** 03-12-1967 to 01-04-1975
9. **Hon'ble Justice Raja Jaswant Singh:** 02-04-1975 to 23-01-1976
10. **Hon'ble Justice M.R.A. Ansari:** 23-01-1976 to 08-11-1977
11. **Hon'ble Justice Mian Jalal-ud-Din:** 15-02-1978 to 22-02-1980
12. **Hon'ble Justice Mufti Baha-ud-Din:** 07-03-1983 to 23-08-1983
13. **Hon'ble Justice V. Angaria Khalid:** 24-08-1983 to 24-06-1984
14. **Hon'ble Dr. Justice Adarsh Sein Anand:** 11-05-1985 to 23-10-1989
15. **Hon'ble Justice S.S. Kang:** 24-10-1989 to 14-05-1993
16. **Hon'ble Justice S.C. Mathur:** 10-10-1993 to 17-03-1994
17. **Hon'ble Justice S. Sagir Ahmed:** 18-03-1994 to 22-09-1994
18. **Hon'ble Justice M. Ramakrishna:** 10-10-1994 to 15-06-1997

19. **Hon'ble Justice Bhawani Singh:** 16-06-1997 to 21-02-2000
20. **Hon'ble Dr. Justice B.P. Sarar:** 21-02-2000 to 22-08-2001
21. **Hon'ble Justice H. K. Sema:** 12-09-2001 to 08-04-2002
22. **Hon'ble Justice BC Patel:** 16-05-2002 to 04-03-2003
23. **Hon'ble Justice Sachchidanand Jha:** 04-02-2004 to 11-10-2005
24. **Hon'ble Shri Justice B. A. Khan:** 25-01-2007 to 31-03-2007
25. **Hon'ble Shri Justice Aftab Alam:** 07-06-2007 to 10-11-2007
26. **Hon'ble Shri Justice K.S. Radhakrishnan:** 07-01-2008 to 28-08-2008
27. **Hon'ble Shri Justice Manmohan Sarin:** 04-09-2008 to 19-10-2008
28. **Hon'ble Shri Justice Barin Ghosh:** 03-01-2009 to 13-04-2010
29. **Hon'ble Shri Justice Aftab Hussain Saikia:** 13-04-2010 to 06-04-2011
30. **Hon'ble Shri Justice F.M. Ibrahim Kalifulla:** 18-09-2011 to 01-04-2012
31. **Hon'ble Justice M.M. Kumar:** 08-06-2012 to January 2015
32. **Hon'ble Justice N. Paul Vasantha Kumar:** 02-02-2015 — 14-03-2017
33. **Hon'ble Justice Badar Durrez Ahmed:** 01-04-2017 — 15-03-2018
34. **Hon'ble Justice Ramaligam Sudhakar:** 16-03-2018 — 11-05-2019
35. **Hon'ble Justice Alok Aradhe (acting):** 11-05-2018 — 11-08-2018

**For Latest Information Refer to Who's Who &
Current Affairs Section in the beginning of the Book**

❑ ❑ ❑

18 Industries

INDUSTRIAL INFRASTRUCTURE

Important Industrial Areas: Industrial Complex, Bari Brahmana, Jammu; Industrial Estate, Gangyal, Jammu; Industrial Growth Centre, Samba, Jammu; Integrated Infrastructure Development Project, Udhampur; Export Promotion Industrial Park, Kartholi, Jammu; Industrial Area, Kathua; Electronic Complex, Rangreth, Srinagar; Industrial Complex Lassipora, Pulwama, Kashmir; Industrial Complex, Khonmoh, Srinagar; Industrial Estate, Zainakote, Srinagar; Industrial Estate, Zakura, Srinagar; Industrial Growth Centre, Ompora, Budgam.

Industrial Estates in Various Districts

S.No.	District	No. of Estates	Area in Kanals	S.No.	District	No. of Estates	Area in Kanals
1.	Srinagar	7	2573.06	8.	Udhampur	2	1100.00
2.	Budgam	2	1249.00	9.	Kathua	3	1161.09
3.	Anantnag	5	387.06	10.	Rajouri	1	52.00
4.	Pulwama	5	7583.00	11.	Poonch	1	26.00
5.	Baramulla	4	195.00	12.	Kargil	1	116.00
6.	Kupwara	2	118.00	13.	Leh	1	500.00
7.	Jammu	6	6485.14		**TOTAL**	**40**	**21545.35**

COTTAGE INDUSTRIES

Jammu Province

1. **Calico Printing (Cotton Printing, Silk Cloth designs):** Samba and Jammu.
2. **Bee Keeping (Honey):** Doda, Ramnagar, Basohali, Bishnah and Udhampur.
3. **Nara Making (Nara):** Smailpur, Bishnah, etc.
4. **Wines (wine etc.):** R.S. Pura, Simbal Camp and Bhore Camp, etc.
5. **Utensil Making (Brass, Copper and Aluminium utensil):** Jammu, Kathua.
6. **Chappals and Shoes (Foot-wear, Tanning and Preparing Leather):** Jammu and Muthi.

19 Tourism

Tourism forms an integral part of the Jammu & Kashmir and Ladakh economy often termed as "Paradise on Earth". Kashmir is famous for its lakes, sweet-water, clear streams. Cool air, mighty mountains and growing number of tourist resorts which attracts the tourists throughout the world.

GENERAL TOURISM IN JAMMU

Katra: 50 kms from Jammu. This small town serves as the base camp for visiting the famous shrine of Vaishnodeviji in the Trikuta Hills. The shrine is approachable on foot along a 12 kms. Long well laid foot-path. Every year, nearly 4 million pilgrims pass through Katra on their way to Vaishnodeviji.

Patnitop: 112 kms from Jammu. This famous hill resort is perched on a beautiful plateau, at an altitude of 2024 metres across which the Jammu-Srinagar Highway passes.

Sanasar: 119 kms. from Jammu and only 17 kms. from Patnitop, Sanasar is cup shaped meadow surrounded by gigantic conifers. A place for a quite holiday, the meadow has now been developed as a golf course. It also provides opportunities for para-gliding.

Batote: 125 kms from Jammu Situated at an altitude of 1560 metres on the Jammu-Srinagar National Highway, this resort straddles the forested slopes of the Patnitop mountain range, overlooking the spectacular lie of the Chenab gorge. This place is a very well developed tourist resort with lots of commercial activity and facilities.

Mantalai: Situated a few kilometers further away from Shud Mahadev, Mantalai is surrounded by lush deodar forests, at an altitude of over 2000 metres. It is believed that Lord Shiva had got married to the Goddess Parvati here.

Mansar Lake: 60 kms. A beautiful lake fringed by forest-covered hills. Boating facilities are available on the spot. Every year around Baisakhi, a food and crafts festival is organised here by J&K Tourism.

Akhnoor: 32 kms. south-west of Jammu situated on the banks of mighty Chenab river is the historic town of Akhnoor. This town is associated with the legend of Soni-Mahiwal. Ruins of the Indus-Valley Civilization are to be seen along the river bank commanding a panoramic view all around.

Dogra Art Gallery: This is located in the erstwhile Pink Hall of the old Mubarak Mandi Palace Complex. This museum houses 800 rare and exquisite paintings from different schools of paintings viz: Basohli, Jammu and Kangra.

PILGRIM TOURISM IN JAMMU

Peer Khoh: A cave shrine located on the circular road, 3.5 kms from the heart of the town. There is a Shiva Lingam formed naturally in the cave; neither its antiquity nor its cause is known. And legend has it that the cave leads underground to many other cave shrines and even out of the country.

Raghunath Temple: Situated in the heart of the city and surrounded by a group of other temples, this temple, dedicated to Lord Rama is outstanding and unique in Northern India. Work on the temple was started by Maharaja Gulab Singh, founder of the Kingdom of Jammu and Kashmir in 1835 AD and was completed by his son Maharaja Ranbir Singh in 1860 AD.

Peer Baba: On the back side of the Civil Airport is famous Dargah of the Muslim saint, Peer Budhan Ali Shah.

Idgah: The city has a number of historic idgah's. Of them Ziarat Baba Buddan Shah is located in the outskirts of Jammu city at a distance of about 8 kms towards the aerodrome at Satwari. This ziarat is very popular among all sections of society and is being visited by large number of people throughout the year. Other idgah's are Ziarat Baba Roshan Shah Wali near Gumat Bazar, Ziarat Peer Mitha near Peer mitha bazar. Another idgah is Panch-Peer.

Gurudwara: The city has a number of historic gurudwara's. Of them Gurudwara Shri Guru Nanak Dev Ji is situated in Upper Bazar near Mubarak Mandi complex. Another Gurudwara's are Talli Sahib near Tallab Tillo and Gurudwara Kalgidhar near Rehari localities of Jammu.

Church: The city has a number of historic churches. Of them Protestant church on Wazarat road is the oldest Church in the city of temples. Other Churches are Roman Catholic Church near Jewel Chowk and Presentation Church of Virgin Mary. Another Church is St. Mary Church on G.L.Dogra road.

Shri Mata Vaishno Devi Shrine: Located at a height of 5300 feet on holy Trikuta Hills. The holy cave shrine of Mata Vaishnodevi Ji is one of the most popular Shrines of the country. The Goddess Vaishnodevi's abode is in a 100 feet long cave with a narrow opening. There are three natural pindies of Maha Saraswati, Maha Lakshmi and Mahakali which represent creative, preservative and destructive aspects of the divine energy. This shrine is 13 kms away from Katra town.

Shahdara Sharief: It is the shrine of Baba Ghulam Shah in the lap of mountains. The shrine, commonly known as Shahdara Sharief is a popular tourist spot in Rajouri district. There was a pir named Ghulam Shah who was born in Syed Family at village Saidian Rawalpindi (now in Pakistan). Ghulam Shah made Shadara his abode for the rest of his life.

Buddha Amarnath: In the north east of Poonch Town is situated an ancient temple of Lord Shiva on the left bank of Pulsata stream. The area is known as Rajpura Mandi, two kms above Mandi village.

Nangali Sahib: Nangali Sahib Gurudwara is situated on the left bank of Drungli Nallah. This Gurudwara was established by Sant Bhai Mela Singh who is said to have visited this shrine in 1810 A.D. when he was on his way to conquer Kashmir.

Bahu Fort/Temple: 5 kms from Jammu city. Situated on a rock face on the left bank of the river Tawi. This is perhaps the oldest fort and edifice in the city. Constructed originally by Raja Bahulochan over 3,000 years ago, the existing Fort was more recently improved and built by Dogra rulers. There is a temple dedicated to Goddess Kali inside the fort popularly known as Bave wali Mata.

GENERAL TOURISM IN KASHMIR

Nishat Garden: Queen Nur-Jehan's brother Asif Khan laid the Garden in 1633 AD. It is situated on the banks of world famous Dal-Lake in the backdrop of Zabarwan hills. This garden commands magnificient view of the lake. The Garden is Terraced with beautiful water channel flowing right in the middle.

Shalimar Garden: This Garden was built by Emperor Jehangir for his beloved wife Nur-Jehan. The Garden has four terraces and is 539x182 meters and gets water from Harwan through canal which is lined with beautiful fountains.

Chashmashahi & Parimahal: Chashmashahi or the Royal spring was laid by Shah Jehan in 1632 AD. It is famous for the spring of refreshing digestive mineral water.

Dal Lake: The world famous water body has been described as Lake Par-Excellence by Sir Walter Lawrence. It is the Jewel in the crown of the Kashmir and is eulogised by poets and praised abundantly by the tourists. The lake is 6x3 kms and is divided in four parts by causeways known as Gagribal, Lokut Dal, Bod Dal and Nagin. The Dal Lake is host to world famous Shikaras and Houseboats which vie with each other with eye catching names.

Harwan: Harwan is huge Garden lined with flower beds and massive Chinar Trees with a beautiful canal flowing right through the middle. The canal is fed from a beautiful lake which lies behind the garden. There is not much clutter of fountains and other fancy things but vast big green carpeted green lawns which form an ideal spot for picnics. This spot is very popular with the locals for picnics and excursions.

Gulmarg: The meadow of Flowers is a world famous tourist spot in the Baramulla district of Kashmir. The altitude of Gulmarg is 2730 meters surrounded by dense forests of tall conifers, Gulmarg is known for unparallel beauty and is rated as one of the matchless tourist spots of the world. It is famous for Golf hikes and boasts of a beautiful highland golf course. It is premier resort for winter sports in the country.

Pahalgam: The Village of nomad is unspoilt by the ravages of progress. This is a quaint little village nestled on the banks of river Lidder. This place is an angler's delight and even an amateur can catch a rainbow trout from the rushing streams. The large brown bear is a natural inhabitant of the thick Pine and Cedar forests. Pahalgam has a golf course at 2400 meters above the sea level. Pahalgam is a base camp for the pilgrims of Amarnath.

Sonamarg: The Golden Meadow is at an altitude of 2740 meters and is gateway to Ladakh. It has brilliant forests of sycamore and alpine flowers, silver birch, fir and pine; Sonamarg is a place of enthralling beauty. Three lakes viz Kishensar, Vishensar and Gangabal can be viewed from Nichnai Pass. 20 kms east of Sonamarg is Zoji-La Pass at 3540 mtrs which leads into Ladakh Plateau.

Wullar Lake: The largest fresh-water lake in India is 60 km from Srinagar. Spreading over a 125 km area, the lake, by drawing off excess water from the Jhelum, acts as a natural flood reservoir. Interesting ruins in the centre of the lake are the remains of an island created by King Zain-ul-abidin. With its turbulent waters perpetually wind ruffled, its exciting variety of avian life and the sheer beauty of its setting, Wullar represents Nature at her most untamed.

PILGRIM TOURISM IN KASHMIR

Amarnath: One of the holy Trinity, Shiva is a living God, the most sacred and the most ancient book of India, the Rigveda evokes his presence in its hymns. Vedic myths, rituals and even astronomy testify to his existence from the dawn of time. But Shiva, Destroyer, the mendicant, is indefinable: He is a great yogi. Legend has it that Shiva recounted to Parvati the secret of creation in a Cave in Amarnath.

Khanqah-e-Moula: The shrine of Shah-e-Hamdan or Khanqah-e-Moul-a is one of the oldest Muslim shrines in Kashmir situated on the banks of river Jhelum in the old city. The shrine was originally constructed by Sultan Sikander (1389-1413 AD) in the memory of Muslim preacher Mir Syed Ali Hamdani who had visited Kashmir and stayed there for meditation and preaching.

Jamia Masjid, Charar-i-sharief, Chhatti Padshahi, Chhatti Padshahi Gurudwara is situated near Srinagar, Kashmir.

Awantipura: The temple ruins at Avantipur represent some of the finest examples of architecture of this region. Dedicated to Vishnu and Shiva, they were built in 9th century AD by King Avantivarman.

GENERAL TOURISM IN LADAKH

Drass: Gate Way to Ladakh: Drass (3230 m), 60 km west of Kargil on the road to Srinagar is a small township lying in the centre of the valley of the same name. It has become famous as the second coldest inhabited place in the world by virtue of the intense cold that descends upon the valley along with repeated snowfalls during winters. Winter temperature is sometimes known to plummet to less than minus 40 degrees.

Kargil: KARGIL (2704 m), 204 kms from Srinagar in the west and 234 kms from Leh in the east, is the second largest urban centre of Ladakh and headquarters of the district of same name. A quite town now, Kargil once served as important trade and transit centre in the Pan-Asian trade network. Numerous caravans carrying exotic merchandise comprising silk, brocade, carpets, felts, tea, poppy, ivory etc. transited in the town on their way to and from China, Tibet, Yarkand and Kashmir.

Excursions: Situated 45 kms East of Kargil on the road to Leh, Mulbek (3230 m) in an area dominated by the Buddhists. It is situated along either banks of the Wakha River, which originates. Many monuments of the early Buddhists era dot the landscape and are accessible from the road.

Mulbek Chamba: The chief attraction of Mulbek is a 9 m high rock sculpture in deep relief of Maitreya, the Future Buddha. Its excursion combines esoteric Shaivite symbolism with early Buddhist art. Situated right on the highway, it dates back to the period when Buddhists missionaries came travelling east of the Himalayas.

Mulbek Gompa: Perched atop a rocky cliff, Mulbek Gompa (monastery) dominates the valley. It is easy to see why in bygone times this site served as an outpost to guard the caravan route. Like all Buddhists monasteries it is adorned by frescoes and statues.

Shergol: Another picturesque village of the Wakha River valley, Shergol is situated across the river, right of the Kargil-Leh road. The main attraction is a cave monastery which is visible from a far as a white speck against the vertically rising ochre hill from which it appears to hang out.

Urgyan Dzong: This meditation retreat lies tucked away in an amazing natural mountain fortress high up in Zanskar range. Concealed within is a circular table land with a small monastic establishment at its centre. The surrounding hillside reveals several caves where high-ranking Buddhists saints meditated in seclusion. At least one such cave is associated with the visit of Padmasambhava, the patron saint of Tibetan Buddhism. The main approach is to footpath laid through the only gap available in the rocky ramparts.

Wakha Rgyal: Tucked away inside the picturesque upper part of the Wakha Valley, upstream of Mulbek, Rgyal gives the appearance of a medieval settlement of cave dwellings transported in to the modern times with some improvements and extensions. The houses, neatly white-washed and closely stacked, are dug into the sheer face of a vertical cliff that rises high above the green valley bottom. From a far the village looks like a colony of beehives hanging from the ochre granite of the Cliffside.

Suru Valley - Sun Snow and Silence: One of the most beautiful regions of Ladakh, the Suru Valley forms the mainstay of Kargil district. Lying nestled along the north-eastern foothills of the great Himalayan Wall, it extends from Kargil town, first southward for a length of about 75 kms upto the expanse around Panikhar, thence eastward for another stretch of nearly 65 kms upto the foot of the Penzila watershed where the Suru valley rises. Its composite population is of about 30,000.

20 Historical Places & Monuments

Martand is a significant Archaeological site. Its impressive Architecture reveals the glorious past of the area. All that remains of the temple is a central rectangular building surrounded by a court and rectangular colonnade. The most important shrine of Amarnath cave is situated about 48 kms from Pahalgam which attracts devotees from all over the world. It is located in the upper reaches of the district at an altitude of about 13000ft from the sea level. Shrine is believed to be an abode of lord Shiva.

The famous shrines of Bab-Zain-Ud-Din Wali is existing at Aishmuqam. The shrine of Baba-Hyder Rishi is located at Anantnag. He is the last giant of Rishi order of saints.

The famous tourist places are Pahalgam, Kokernag, Acchabal, Verinag and Daksum.

Pattan : This is an old town and remained capital of Kashmir during Shankervarman regime. It is 26 kms from Srinagar.

The Tourist Places are Gulmarg, Manasbal Lake, Watlab, Kishan Ganag, Wullar Lake, Sopore, etc.

Tomb of Sheikh Noor-ud-din-Noorani : The tomb of Alamdar-e-Kashmir is situated 28 kms in southwest of Srinagar at Charar-e-Sharif in Budgam District. The shrine on the burial site was constructed by the then ruler of Kashmir Zain ul Abideen. Sheikh Noor-ud-din was born in Kaimoh and his ancestors belonged to Kishtwar. He was a pious soul and travelled throughout Kashmir to spread the message of his religion. He meditated for 12 years inside a cave. Four centuries after his death Afghan governor Atta Mohd. Khan issued coins in his name. The shrine alongwith Khanqah was gutted in a devastating fire in 1995.

The Shrine of Khan Saheb : It is situated in the Khan saheb block of the District. It is associated with famous saint Hazrat Saleh Khan who belonged to village Pakhla of Pakistan. Syed Saleh Khan also meditated inside a cave for 12 years and stayed in Srinagar for some time. He was also a fine calligrapher.

Imam Bara Budgam : The Imambara is a holy place for Shiiete Muslims of Kashmir. This building was constructed in the year 1857. The present imambara is octagonal and has five main entrances each of 12ft width. One of the doors is reserved for women. The Imambara is a piece of indo-Iranian architecture and commands great reverence among Shia masses.

Ziarat Alamdar-E-Kashmir : The land of Khag was fortunate enough to have Sheikh noor-Ud-Din as a visitor. Sheikh selected a rock a Khag for meditation and this bears the imprints of his feet. This rock is known as shah Kaen. A shrine is built there in the memory of the saint.

The Tomb of Sham Ded : Sham ded was a daughter of a Iron smith in Poshker village and was initiated into spirituality by Sheikh-ul-Alam. The pious lady after his death was laid to rest in Poshker village and a shrine was constructed there. Other shrines of various pious saints abound in Budgam. These are shrines of : Baba Latif-ud-Din, Syed Mohd. Samri, Hazrat Ganga Baba Rishi, Zia -ud-Din Bukhari.

The famous Tourist Places are – Nilnag, Yusmarg, Sange-safed, Mount Tutakuti and Tosaimaidan etc.

Bahu Fort is a renowned historical temple of Goddess Mahakali popularly known as Bawe-Wali Mata. The fort overlooks the river Tawi flowing placidly down the Jammu City.

Mubarak Mandi Complex : The complex is housing 76 government offices and courts. The complex has a history as old as 150 years back. It was a royal residence of Dogra rulers. The palaces are built as a group of buildings around the courtyard. Successive Dogra rulers added to the complex in size. The buildings were used as the residences of the royal Dogra families. The complex has halls and galleries which were used for official functions and public events.

Rani Charak Mahal : Rani Charak Mahal is also located on river side, connected with Toshakhana on one side.

Ziarat Baba Buddan Shah : Located in the outskirts of Jammu city at a distance of about 8 kms towards the aerodrome at Satwari. This shrine is very popular among all sections of society. Baba Buddan Shah was borne at Talwandi in Punjab, and it is said that another shrine of this Peer is located at Anandpur Sahib in Punjab.

Ziarat Peer Mitha : In the heart of Jammu city we find a magnificent tomb alongwith a mosque. The Ziarat is popularly known as Peer Mitha. Even the locality around it is named after the Ziarat. The ziarat became popular among the masses as Pir Mitha as he accepted a pinch of sugar among the offerings.

Paanch Peer : This dargah is situated at a little distance from the Maharaja's palace on the Jammu-Srinagar National Highway. The place is as known because of the residence of five peers (holymen), lived here and dedicated themselves to the meditation.

Dargah Garib Shah : This dargah is located at Samba. The Peer had immense spiritual powers and he is included in those Muslim saints who had a large number of devotees from all the faiths and religions. Garib Shah's samadhi is looked after by the local hindus.

Peer Khoh : This cave shrine of Lord Shiva also known as Jamawant cave is said to be the oldest historic place in the Shivalik region. Located amidst Igneous rocks and acacia jungle in North-East of Jammu city on the side of circular road above Tawi river, the history of the cave is said to be connected with epic-age.

Raghunath Temple : Located in the heart of Jammu city, this complex is the most splendid temple complex in Northern India. The main commercial market of Jammu is named after the temple complex. The complex consists of 17 temples. However, it was named after the main temple of Lord Rama, Sita Mata and Lakshman as the Dogra dynasty is believed to be the descendant of Lord Rama. There is hardly any image of deity which is not represented in the temple complex.

Ranbireshwar Temple : It is the biggest Shiva temple in North India. Got constructed by the Dogra rulers, this temple has the biggest Lingam of 7 ft in black stone. In two big halls, there are 1.25 lakh "bona Lingam" brought from Narmadda. There are huge images of Ganesha, Kartikeya and Nandi Bull. This temple was constructed by Maharaja Ranbir Singh.

Purmandal : It is about 40 kms from Jammu city. It is called little Kashi and is located on the banks of holy Devika river considered as sacred as Ganges. Large number of people visit the place on Shivratri and Chaitra Chaurdashi.

Gurudwara Sh. Guru Nanak Devji : It is situated in upper bazaar near mubarak mandi complex. It has 3ft tall white coloured marble statue of guru Nank Devji. Maharana Partap Singh is said to have installed the statue.

Jasrota : It was founded by Raja Jas Dev of Jammu in 1019 A.D. Jasrotias ruled this state upto 1834 A.D., when it was given to Raja Hira Singh.

Mankote : It was founded by Raja Manak Dev, a contemporary of Raja Narsingh Dev of Jammu(1272-1314 A.D.). It was renamed by Raja Suchet Singh (1822-43) as Ramkote.

Lakhanpur : Raja Sangram Singh, founded Lakhanpur state. Lakhanapur is known as the gateway of Jammu & Kashmir.

Bhadu : A prominent town of Billawar tehsil. Bhadu town is situated on Bhini nallah, a tributary of Ujh river.

Tirikote : Near Jasrota and Jandi near Hiranagar were also important states/ principalities in the district.

The Tourist Places are Basholi, Sarthal, Bani, Billwar, Ujh, Banjal, Sukarala Mata, Peer Fazal Shah, Dhar Mahanpur and Banjal etc.

The Payer Temple : Payer temple is situated about 3 kms in the south of Pulwama district. The temple is known after the village, Payer, where it is situated. Vigne, Cunningham and some other travellers call it Payech temple.

Asar Sharief Pintoora : The shrine is the most revered religious place in the district situated 12 kms from Pulwama. The shrine houses the holy relic of Prophet Mohammed (Peace Be Upon Him) which is displayed on special occasions associated with the life of the Prophet(PBUH).

The shrine of Shah Hamdan : It is situated in Tral town, the shrine is believed to have been built by Mir Syed Ali Hamdani. People in large numbers throng the shrine on annual festivals associated with the saint.

Tourist Places : The Pulwama district has some beautiful tourist spots, the famous among which are: Aharbal, Nagberan, Shikargah, Tarsar Marsar, Kungwattan and Hurpora, etc.

Ramkund : Another well known shrine located about 68 kms from Poonch town is that of Ram Kund. Believed to be of Mahabharat period, it is just 11 kms away from Mendhar. The Kund was said to be constructed by Raja Lalitaditya while others believe that Raja renovated it, and originally it was constructed by Lord Rama when he was on his way to Kashmir. There are three springs. People take bath on first of bright half of Chaitra.

Ziarat Sain : Situated in village Guntrian, 10 kms from Poonch, the Ziarat of saint Sain Mira Sahib is a popular pilgrim centre, hundreds of devotees visit this Ziarat.

Ziarat Chhotay Sahib : Located 58 kms away from Poonch and 4 kms from Mendhar this Ziarat is situated in the village Sakhimaidan. Hundreds of pilgrims come to this place every day.

Thanamandi : This is an important historical place from the time of Mughals who used to stay here during journey from Delhi to Kashmir and vice versa. The climate of this place is very charming and infact a health resort. It is also famous for its artistic wooden products. The famous shrine of Shahdara Shariaf is 6 kms from this place.

Dhandidhar Fort : It is a historical monument located on a hill in the vicinity of Rajouri town. This fort was probably constructed by Mughal King during the reign of Emperor Jahangir nearly 400 years back. It is just 2 kms away from Rajouri presenting panoramic and impressive view of the entire area.

War Memorial : It has been raised at Gujjar Mandi Chowk in Rajouri township. Rajouri was liberated by the Indian army on 13th April 1948. Major General Kulwant Singh launched an attack against Pakistani forces who had converted the site of present airfield into a slaughter ground.

Hall of Fame : On the top of the mound, the great memorial Hall of Fame has been constructed in commemoration of the heroic deeds of those who had laid down their lives for the sake of their motherland in the sectors of Rajouri and Poonch.

Hazratbal Shrine : The Hazrathalbal Shrine, which is situated on the left bank of the famous Dal Lake is in Srinagar. This unmatched reverence is anchored in the love and respect for the Prophet Mohammad (peace be upon him), whose Moi-e-Muqqadas, (the sacred hair) is preserved here. The shrine is known by many names including Hazrathbal, Assar-e-Sharief, Madinat-us-Sani, Dargah Sharief and Dargah. Sadiq Khan laid out a garden here and constructed a palatial building, Ishrat mahal or Pleasure House, in 1623. The construction of the present marble structure was started by the Muslim Aquaf Trust headed by Sheikh Mohammad Abdullah in 1968 and completed in 1979.The Moi-e-Muqqadas is displayed on various occasions related with the life of the Prophet and his four holy companions.

Shankaracharya Temple : It is located at 1100 ft above surface level of the main city on the Shankaracharya hill, also known as Takht-e-Suleiman. The Shiva temple, as Kalhana believes, was constructed by Raja Gopadatya in 371 B.C. and as such is the oldest shrine in Kashmir. Dogra ruler, Maharaja Gulab Singh, constructed stone stairs upto the temple. In 1925, the temple was electrified. The temple, besides a prominent religious place of Hindus, is of great archaeological importance. The temple commands a magnificent panoramic view of the Srinagar city.

Jama Masjid : It is one of the oldest and the most spacious of all the mosques in Kashmir, situated in the heart of the city. The foundation of the mosque, an architectural wonder was laid by Sultan Sikander in 1398 A.D. The area of the mosque is 384 ft × 381 ft spacious enough for over thirty thousand people to offer prayers at a time.

LADAKH (UT)

Hemis: Situated 40 kms from Leh, Hemis is the wealthiest, best known and biggest gompa of Ladakh. The annual festival of the gompa is held in summer in honour of Guru Padma Sambhav's birth anniversary. It also has the largest thanka (scroll painting on silk or brocade) in Ladakh which is unfurled once in 12 years. Hemis was built in 1630 A.D. during the reign of Sengge Namgyal and flourished under the Namgyal dynasty.

Alchi: The gompa is situated on the banks of the Indus, 70 kms from Leh and dates a thousand years back. The gompa is no longer an active religious centre and is looked after by monks from the Likir monastery.

Spituk: The gompa stands prominently on the top of a hillock, 8 kms from Leh, and commands a panoramic view of the Indus Valley for miles. Many icons of Buddha and five thankas are found in 15th century monastery. There is also a collection of ancient masks, antique arms, and an awe inspiring image of Mahakal.

Phyang: The monastery is situated 17 kms from Leh on the Leh-Kargil road. It was built by Tashi Namgyal in the later half of the 16th century A.D. and looks like a place from a distance. The gompa belongs to the Red Cap sect of the Buddhists. Hundreds of icons of Buddha are kept on wooden shelves.

Shey: 15 kms upstream from Leh the palace is believed to have been the seat of power of the pre-Tibetan kings. A 7.5 metre high copper statue of Buddha, plated with gold, and the largest of its kind, is installed in the palace.

Thikse: The Thikse monastery is spectacularly situated 19 kms from Leh. It is one of the largest and architecturally most impressive gompas. The gompa has images, stupas and wall paintings of Buddha which are exquisite.

Jama Masjid: The historical mosque is situated in the heart of Leh town. It was built in 1666-67 A.D. consequent to an agreement between the Mughal Emperor Aurangzeb and then ruler of Ladakh, Deldan Namgyal.

Leh Palace: The palace is a distinguished monument and a historical building. The nine-storeyed palace was built by the 17th century illustrious ruler of Ladakh Sengge Namgyal. ❑ ❑ ❑

21 ▸ Important Personalities

Jammu-Kashmir and Ladakh are unique in many senses and its citizen show their brilliance in various fields. Some noted among them are:

AMAR NATH KAK

Amar Nath Kak was a prominent Kashmiri lawyer and author. His most important books are 'Hamara Vrittanta' and 'the Gayatri', both written in Hindi. He was the elder brother of Kashmiri archaeologist and politician Ram Chandra Kak. 'Hamara Vrittanta' is a mine of information on the social and religious life of Kashmiri Pandits in the first half of the 20th century. It also presents the drama of the war between India and Pakistan.

ANUPAM KHER

Anupam Kher is an established actor of Hindi films. He is a Kashmiri Brahmin. He has acted in nearly two hundred Bollywood films including several English films.

ABDUL GHANI LONE

Abdul Ghani Lone was a lawyer turns politician who for most of his professional career worked as Kashmiri separatist. He was assassinated on May 21, 2002, while commemorating the 12th anniversary of the Kashmiri leader, Mirwaiz Maulvi Farooq. He made his first entry into politics serving in the state assembly as a Congress candidate in 1967. In 1978, he formed a Kashmir separatist organization called the 'People's Conference' dedicated to "the restoration of 'internal autonomy' in Kashmir".

AYATOLLAH AGHA SYED YOUSUF AL-MOOSAVI

Ayotollah Agha Syed Yousuf Al-Moosavi was a Kashmiri religious scholar and leader of Shia sect of Muslims. He founded the 'Anjuman-e-Sharia' organization which remains influential under his successors. Agha sahib, as he was popularly known, was a charismatic leader, a social reformer, a visionary, an educationist, a scholar.

DINANATH NADIM

Dinanath Nadim was a prominent Kashmiri poet of 20th century. With Dinanath Nadim's poetry, a new phase was introduced in Kashmiri various poetic styles into Kashmiri. He was the first Kashmiri poet to write in 'blank verse'. He used the Kashmiri language with great grace and craftsmanship. He depicted the beauty, the poverty and the plight of Kashmir in his poetry. Nadim has also composed poetry in folk style. In 1971, He received the Soviet Land Nehru Award (1971) and the Sahitya Natak Academy Award (1986) for his book 'Shihil Kul' (poetry).

FAROOQ ABDULLAH

Farooq Abdullah is the son of Sheikh Abdullah and has served as Chief Minister of Jammu & Kashmir on several occasions since 1982. He was also a cabinet minister in Manmohan Singh government.

GHULAM RASOOL SANTOSH

Gulam Rasool Santosh was a prominent Kashmiri painter. He was best known for his themes inspired by 'Kashmir Shaivism'. His paintings are known for the vibrancy of colours, neat lines, spiritual energy and sensuousness. Santosh also wrote plays, poetry and essays in Kashmiri language.

GULAM NABI AZAD

Gulam Nabi Azad is a politician from the Indian National Congress. He was the Parliamentary Affairs Minister of India in the Manmohan Singh goverment until October 27, 2005, when he was appointed as the Chief Minister of Jammu & Kashmir. Now, he is Leader of opposition in Rajya Sabha.

JAFFER ALI

Jaffer Ali was a world-renowned papier-mache artist and entrepreneur from Hussanabad. Srinagar, Kashmir, Jaffer Ali received numerous awards, including one from Indian Prime Minister Indira Gandhi, for his exemplary work in promoting Kashmiri handicrafts. His skills in the art descended through his grandfather who brought the papier-mache trade to Kashmir from Mashad, Iran.

KALHANA

Kalhana, a Kashmiri Brahmin was the celebrated author of 'Rajatarangini' based on Kashmiri history. He wrote this book during AD 1147-49. Kalhana is regarded to be Kashmir's first historian. 'Rajatarangini' is one of the most valuable sources of Indian history.

KSHEMRAJA

Kshemraja was a philosopher and a disciple of Abhinav Gupta. He wrote original works of 'Kashmir Shaivism'.

MEHRAJUDDIN WADOO

Mehrajuddin Wadoo is a footbal player of the state. He is currently playing for the Indian national team. At the club level, he plays for East Bengal. Mehrajuddin started out as a striker but then shifted to the defence, now he has leapt to the midfield position, where his stature came to help him settle in . He started out with Jammu & Kashmir Police and with the pasage of time boarded HAL, ITI, Sporting Club de Goa, Mohun Bagan and now for East Bengal.

MUFTI MOHAMMAD SAYEED

Mufti Mohammad Sayeed was a politician in Jammu & Kashmir who was the Chief Minister from 2002 until 2005 and from 2015 to 2016. He leads the People's Democratic Party (PDP), a Jammu & Kashmir based party which he formed in July, 1999, to persuade the Government of India to initiate an unconditional dialogue with Kashmiris for resolution of the Kashmir problem. He died on January 7, 2016.

MEHBOOBA MUFTI SAYEED

Mehbooba Mufti Sayeed is the Current and 13th CM of Jammu & Kashmir. She is the daughter of Mufti Mohammad Sayeed, former Chief Minister of Jammu & Kashmir.

MJ AKBAR

MJ Akbar is a leading journalist and author. He is the founder and former editor-in-chief and managing director of 'The Asian Age'. He has written several non-fiction books. He was External Affairs minister of State in Narendra Modi government.

MUZAMMIL IBRAHIM

Muzammil Ibrahim is a model, originally from state of Jammu & Kashmir. He won the Gladrags Manhunt Contest in 2003. He also won the Rashtrapati Award for bravery (1994) for saving a boy from drowning in 1992.

OMAR ABDULLAH

Omar Abdullah is the son of Farooq Abdullah and grandson of Shiekh Abdullah. He was minister in Atal Behari Vajpayee's government. He was re-elected as President of National Conference for a 2nd term in 2006. He is the former chief minister of Jammu & Kashmir.

PRAN KISHORE KAUL

Pran Kishore Kaul is a famous Kashmiri stage personality. In addition to acting, he has directed and written screenplays. He was bestowed an award from the Sahitya Natak Academy for his novel Sheen TV Walu Pod. He was one of the founders of the Miltsar Kashmir Music and Dance Group, a group that travels widely with the goal of supporting Kashmiri and Indian arts.

PANDIT BHAJAN SOPORI

Pandit Bhajan Sopori is a Hindustani instrumental composer from Kashmir. Santoor maestro, Pandi Bhajan Sopori comes from a family of musicians of 'Sufiyana Gharana' of Kashmir and Santoor is what he inherited from his predecessors. He has performed for leading cultural association, Radio Sangeet Sammelans and other National Programmes of Radio and Doordarshan and has received many awards of merit for his musical excellence. Shir Bhajan Sopori is also a music director of repute having produced several musical productions and has composed music for songs in various Indian languages. He has also composed music for operas, telefilms, serials and documentaries.

PN DHAR

PN Dhar was Principal Secretary to Mrs. Indira Gandhi Prime Minister's office during the tumultuous days of the Emergency (1973-77) and, therefore, he had much influence in the unfolding of those events. He was also a professor of Economics at Delhi University, and for many years Director of the Institute of Economic Growth.

SWAMI LAKSHMAN JOO

Swami Lakshman Joo was a famed mystic and scholar of 'Kashmir Shaivism'. He was known as 'Lal Sahib' or 'Friend of God' by followers and considered by them to be a fully realized saint.

SHEIKH MOHAMMED ABDULLAH

Shiekh Mohammed Abdullah popularly known as 'Sher-e-Kashmir' was the leader of the National Conference, Kashmir's largest political party, and one of the most important plitical figures in the modern history of Jammu & Kashmir. He did his Masters in Chemistry and joined Government Service as teacher, but later resigned and spearheaded popular movement for democratic rights of people, founding the Muslim Conference (name, later changed to National Conference) in AD 1931. He agitated against the rule of the Maharaja Hari Singh, and urged self-rule for Kashmir.

He was the Prime Minister of Jammu & Kashmir State soon after its controversial provisional accession to India in 1947, and was later jailed and exiled. He again became the Chief Minister of the State following 1974 Indira-Sheikh accord and remained in the top slot still his death on September 8, 1982.

SYED MIR QASIM

Syed Mir Qasim was the Chief Minister of Kashmir during AD 1971-75 and well respected throughout India as a gentleman politician and statesman. Former Indian Prime Minister Dr. Manmohan Singh described Syed Mir Qasim as a 'great nationalist who worked selflessly in public interest and for peace and development in Jammu & Kashmir'.

Syed Mir Qasim's political career first began during India's freedom struggle against Britain, when he became a leader of the non-sectarian, pro-democracy Quit Kashmir political movement. His advocacy against monarchical rule resulted in his imprisonment as a political prisoner by the Maharaja of Kashmir, Hari Singh. After India's independence, Syed Mir Qasim drafted the Kashmiri Constitution and went on to serve in various State and Union positions. Syed Mir Qasim most famously offered to resign from the Chief Ministership in order to encourage and institutionalize the landmark Indira Gandhi-Sheikh Abdullah Accord in AD 1975. He was posthumously awarded India's highest civilian award in AD 2005.

Spiritual Personalities

- Sheikh-ul- Alam Alamdar-e-Kashmir- Charari Sharief Kashmir
- Sheikh Hamza Makhdoomi Kashmiri.-Srinagar, Kashmir
- Syed Baha-ud-Din Naqshband.-Srinagar. Kashmir.
- Shah Asrar-ud-Din-Kishtawar, Jammu.
- Syed Janbaz Wali-Khanpura, Baramula.
- Syed Yaqoob Saheb-Srinagar, Kashmir.
- Baba Payam-ud-Din Reshi- Gulmarg, Kashmir.
- Bul Bul Shah-Bulbul Lanker, Kashmir.
- Syed Mirak Shah Kashani-Srinagar, Kashmir.
- Mata Vaishno Devi-Katra, Jammu.
- Mata Sharika Devi-Hariparbat-Kashmir
- Mata Ropa Bhavani-Kashmir.

Mirwaiz (Top Religious Seat)

- Mirwaiz Moulvi Ghulam Ahmad
- Mirwaiz Moulvi Ghulam Rasool
- Mirwaiz Moulvi Yousuf Shah
- Mirwaiz Moulvi Muhammad Farooq
- Mirwaiz Moulvi Umer Farooq

Philosophers

- Anandavardhana
- Kshemaraja
- Krishnadasa
- Abhinavagupta
- Somananda
- Bhatta Kallata
- Bhaskara
- Vasugupta
- Utpaladeva

Historians

- Kalhana, 12th century
- Shrivara, 15th century
- Gopi Krishna, 17th century
- Jonaraja, 15th century
- Prajna Bhatta, 16th century
- Swami Lakshman Joo, 17th century
- Hassan Shah Kashmiri, 18th century

Politicians

- Padma Sachdev
- Jawaharlal Nehru, First prime minister of India
- Indira Gandhi, Prime minister of India, daughter of Jawaharlal Nehru
- Rajiv Gandhi, Prime minister of India, son of Indira Gandhi, grandson of Jawaharlal Nehru
- Ghulam Ahmad Ashai, Educationist, Leader and Reformist
- Tej Bahadur Sapru, Politician and lawyer
- Kailash Nath Katju, Politician and lawyer
- Ram Chandra Kak, Archaeologist and politician
- Mohammad Shafi Qureshi, Ex Governor Bihar and Madhya Pradesh, Minister of State Railways India.
- Shaikh Abdullah, Prime Minister and Chief Minister of J&K.
- Syed Mir Qasim, Chief Minister, J&K.

Film Makers

- Arun Kaul
- Ved Rahi
- Sanjay Kak
- Sagar Sarhadi
- Siddharth Kak
- Mani Kaul
- Vidhu Vinod Chopra.
- Ashok Pandit

Leading Journalists and Columnists

- Mulkh Raj Saraf- Father of Journalism in J&K
- Rashid Taseer
- Khwaja Sonaullah Bhat.
- Ghulam Nabi Khayal
- Shamim Ahmad Shamim
- Ahmad Ali Fayaz
- Tariq Bhat
- Lalit Kaul
- Bashir Ahmed Bashir
- Altaf Hussain
- Haroon Rasheed
- Majid Jehangeer
- Aijaz ul Haq
- Syed Ali Safvi
- Bilal Bhat
- Nazir Masoodi
- Syeda Atshana
- Bilal Waza
- Sofi Mohi-ud-Din.
- Ved Bhasin
- Sofi Ghulam Muhammad.
- Muhammad Shaban Vakil
- Muzamil Jaleel
- Sameer Kaul
- M.K.Teng
- Yusuf Jameel
- Zaffar Meraj
- Bansi Pandit
- Ahsan ul Haque
- Riyaz Wani
- Naseer Ahmad
- Mufti Islah
- Showkat Mota
- Muhammad Sidiq
- Sameer Arshad

◄22► Population

Sl. No.	State/ District	Total Population			Sex-Ratio	Population Density
		Males	Females	Total	2011	2011
	J& K	**66,40,662**	**59,00,640**	**1,25,41,302**	**889**	**124**
1.	Jammu	8,13,821	7,16,137	15,29,958	880	678
2.	Srinagar	6,51,124	5,85,705	12,36,829	900	613
3.	Anantanag	5,59,767	5,18,925	10,78,692	927	306
4.	Baramula	5,34,733	4,73,306	10,08,039	885	240
5.	Kupwara	4,74,190	3,96,164	8,70,354	835	366
6.	Badgam	3,98,041	3,55,704	7,53,745	894	554
7.	Rajauri	3,45,351	2,97,064	6,42,415	860	244
8.	Kathua	3,26,109	2,90,326	6,16,435	890	246
9.	Pulwama	2,93,064	2,67,376	5,60,440	912	516
10.	Udhampur	2,96,784	2,58,201	5,54,985	870	211
11.	Poonch	2,51,899	2,24,936	4,76,835	893	285
12.	Kulgam	2,17,620	2,06,863	4,24,483	951	929
13.	Doda	2,13,641	1,96,295	4,09,936	919	46
14.	Bandipore	2,07,680	1,84,552	3,92,232	889	1137
15.	Samba	1,69,124	1,49,774	3,18,898	886	319
16.	Reasi	1,66,461	1,48,206	3,14,667	890	183
17.	Ganderbal	1,58,720	1,38,726	2,97,446	874	1153
18.	Ramban	1,49,132	1,34,581	2,83,713	902	213
19.	Shopian	1,36,480	1,29,735	2,66,215	951	853
20.	Kishtwar	1,20,165	1,10,531	2,30,696	920	140
21.	Kargil	77,785	63,017	1,40,802	810	10
22.	Leh (Ladakh)	78,971	54,516	1,33,487	690	3